ON THE ALTAR
DEDICATE

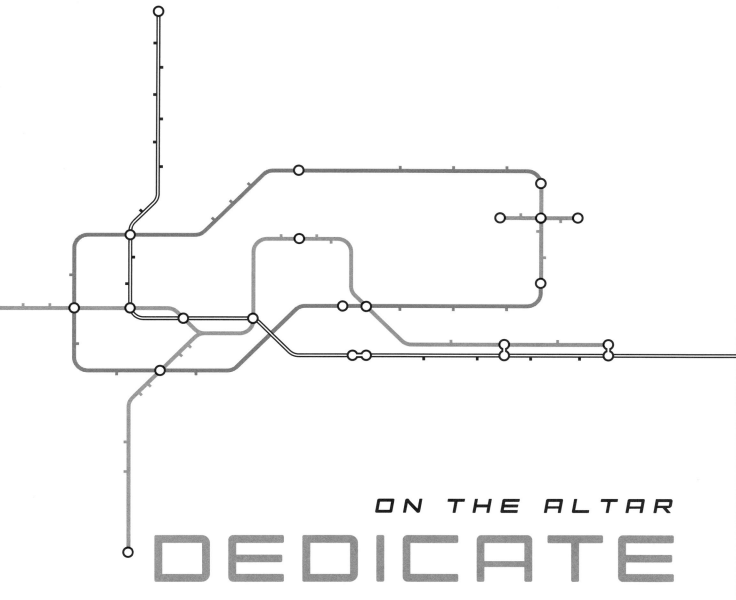

ON THE ALTAR
DEDICATE
14 EVENT-DRIVEN STUDENT MINISTRY OUTLINES

GARTH HECKMAN

Standard®
PUBLISHING
Bringing The Word to Life

Published by Standard Publishing, Cincinnati, Ohio
www.standardpub.com

Also available: On the Altar: *Surrender*

Printed in the United States of America

Project editor: Robert Irvin
Cover and interior design: The DesignWorks Group

ISBN 978-0-7847-2266-4

15 14 13 12 11 10 09   9 8 7 6 5 4 3 2 1

CONTENTS

LET'S GET IT STARTED

As a youth pastor or youth leader, how often have you had these thoughts while putting together a meeting for your group? *If I just had more time.* Or, *If I just knew how to make it stick.* You want to provide something life-changing for your students, but you also have to do it in the midst of your own crazy-busy life.

We're here to help! The On the Altar books—starting with this book, *Dedicate*, and its companion volume, *Surrender*—not only give you proven outlines and relevant applications, both with a scriptural basis, they provide opportunities for memorable experiences at the beginning and end of every youth talk.

When was the last time one of your youth meetings had your students talking about and living out, and not just *hearing*, what you said? This book is about helping you get your students to the point of laying their lives at the altar.

HOW DOES IT WORK?

Each book has outlines for fourteen fantastic youth meetings. You'll have enough for a quarter's worth of meetings and an extra one to spare.

We've broken this book into two halves. Both follow the *Dedicate* theme: The first seven meetings will help your students grasp God's plan to bring them to a life of **discipleship** to Jesus Christ; the second seven, building off that foundation, are meetings on how God wants the very best for them, a life of **fulfillment** in Christ (as shown by Jesus' words in John 10:10).

Each session starts with an icebreaker (Get It Started) that will get your students up and moving. And, in following the theme of that meeting, this activity will put them in the right frame of mind. Most of all, they're a blast! In this section, a short list (What's Needed) is provided so you can prep beforehand the things needed to make it happen. While we've given you the prep list and how-to-do-it, we encourage you to make these activities work, to make them as fun as they can be, for your group. You're a youth leader; hey, by definition you're a highly resourceful person!

After reviewing the Scripture passage that is the foundation for that meeting, we've given you a great youth talk. Again, it can't be stressed enough that, though these are outlined for you, including the text for an entire talk, you should make these *your* messages. Adjust, adapt, add, or subtract; you know what works best for your group!

We've built in For Discussion questions in different places in each unit for lots of group participation.

Another feature of these books is that we've provided places throughout these talks for you to add in your stories, style, and unique voice. We call this the Burst and Branded section.

BURST AND BRANDED

Don't worry—no one gets hurt. The idea behind this element—we've provided one Burst and Branded, on average, per every major outlined point—is simple. But it's also a key ingredient in making each talk yours, in really owning these lessons.

Burst: At this spot in the outline, add your own burst of ideas that speak directly to that part of the lesson. Maybe you have a great personal story, or a story from a friend, to bring this to life. Maybe it's a story you found online, in your local newspaper, or from one of your students' school experiences.

Branded: Here you really put some teeth into each section. How has this particular point changed you or someone you know? The key here is real, lasting change, the kind that impacts for life. These types of stories make your talks more real because your students will relate to you and see you as vulnerable.

Don't feel like you have to fill out each one of these in every section; they're there for when inspiration strikes. And though we had to put them somewhere on the page, plug in your stories wherever they work best. In other words, feel free to move your Burst and Branded stories around.

Last, in each of the outlines, certain areas have been underlined; these are particular points to pay attention to that will help you challenge your students throughout the meeting.

The Wrap It Up sections then provide a link to the closing activity, in which you'll leave your students altered . . .

WALK ON DOWN

From antiquity, altars have been sacred places of worship. In ancient times, they were used for actual sacrifices or some other means of bowing before God. More recently, they're places of worship such as the Communion table.

Maybe you have an altar area in your youth room. Maybe you just have an area near the front where you have the speaker's stand or a stage where a worship band plays. Whatever the case, the idea is to set up an area in which your students can come forward to get their hearts closer to God.

The idea behind the Altered activity is *not* to set up "altar calls" for students to come forward to give their lives to Christ—though at times that may happen. What each one *is* about is to get kids talking, remembering, and *acting on* what they've just heard. They'll leave your students with a spiritual buzz and something they'll be talking about the next day at school. And hey, these activities just might help your group grow numerically as well as spiritually.

For each Altered, we've given you a short list of things needed to make it happen. But again: These student events are yours; adapt the activities to what will work best for your group.

Along the way, we've added various ministry ideas or other options for the Get It Started or Altered activities that may work for your group.

A FINAL WORD

Take some time to go over each lesson in advance, digest them, and add your own insights. And don't worry: we've worked hard at making these as cheap as possible—we know what most youth budgets look like (pretty similar to your checkbook).

Get everything in place for the meeting, spend some time praying for the students God's going to bring out, and create an atmosphere where life-change can happen.

Most of all, have fun. And trust in the one who can leave your students permanently altered!

The activities in this book are designed for learning and having fun (a novel concept—we know), but student participation should *always* be voluntary. It is not the intention of the author or publisher that harm should come to anyone involved in these activities. (Another shocking statement . . .) Neither may be held responsible should someone become ill or injured from participating. (But hey, you're a youth leader, and despite all the crazy stereotypes, we're sure you won't let that happen!)

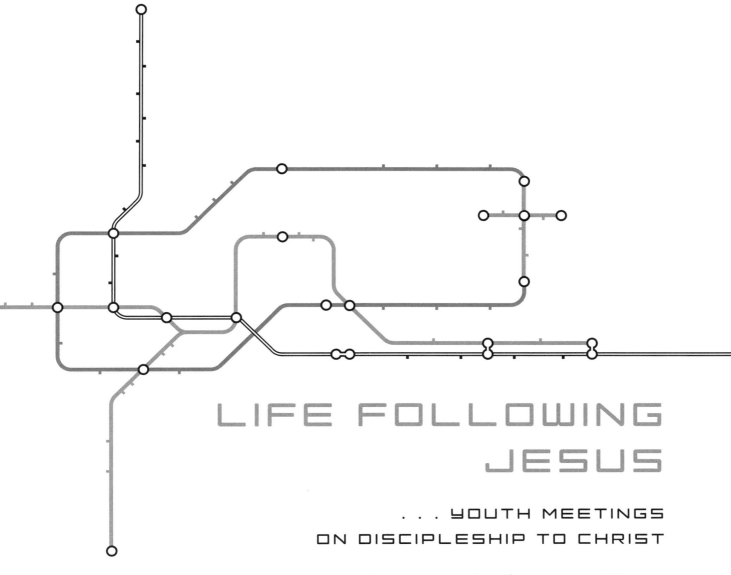

LIFE FOLLOWING
JESUS

. . . YOUTH MEETINGS
ON DISCIPLESHIP TO CHRIST

Therefore, I urge you, brothers, in view of God's mercy, to offer your
bodies as living sacrifices, holy and pleasing to God—this is your
spiritual act of worship. Do not conform any longer to the pattern of this
world, but be transformed by the renewing of your mind.
Then you will be able to test and approve what God's will is—
his good, pleasing and perfect will.

– Romans 12:1, 2

"If anyone would come after me, he must deny himself
and take up his cross daily and follow me."

– Luke 9:23

TOUCH THE HEM
(WHATEVER IT TAKES)

WHAT IT'S ALL ABOUT

Have you ever had the chance to shake a famous person's hand? Most people have had one of those "brush with fame" stories, right? But honestly, did anything truly magical happen for you? Other than maybe a few goose bumps or a quick photo op, you probably didn't come away changed.

But what if you could touch Jesus on a daily basis? What about your students? Would it change you? Them? In fact, we can. We just have to have the same heart as a certain woman in the Bible. This youth talk shows us that we can make, and keep, a daily appointment to touch the life of Jesus.

Get It Started

What's needed: This is an easy one to set up (you're welcome!): a *blindfold;* and *items of your choosing* to play this little game (below) with: your list might include things like a feather, ice cube, guitar pick, dirty sock, match, maybe even a small animal that won't squirm too much—just think fun!

Play "What just touched me?" Ask students to volunteer to sit in a chair up front and be blindfolded. Then touch his or her face or under-forearm (*only* these areas) with different objects and see if they can guess what the item is. Use any of the items from the list above, or others. It's a blast for the other students to watch their friend try to guess what the item is.

Where It's Found in the Bible

Luke 8:42-48

As Jesus was on his way, the crowds almost crushed him. And a woman was there who had been subject to bleeding for twelve years, but no one could heal her. She came up behind him and touched the edge of his cloak, and immediately her bleeding stopped.

"Who touched me?" Jesus asked.

When they all denied it, Peter said, "Master, the people are crowding and pressing against you."

But Jesus said, "Someone touched me; I know that power has gone out from me."

Then the woman, seeing that she could not go unnoticed, came trembling and fell at his feet. In the presence of all the people, she told why she had touched him and how she had been instantly healed. Then he said to her, "Daughter, your faith has healed you. Go in peace."

YOUTH TALK OUTLINE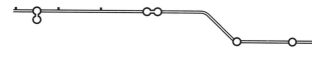

1. Great Expectations

a. What are you reaching for?

It's happened to all of us. You're desperately trying to reach something and you just can't seem to put your hand on it. Maybe it's your cell phone that's fallen between the seats of your car, or some dollar bills, or maybe you're trying to dig some change out of the couch. Or it could be something really important like the edge of a boat just after it turns over or the railing as you begin to fall down the stairs. All you need is one good hand on that thing and everything will be OK. From day to day we're all reaching for something in life.

We reach for friends, good grades, a car, for money to put gas in our car! Or, more deeply, we reach for meaning in our lives. No matter who we are we're all reaching—and many times we're unsuccessful in getting what we want. There are times we find that even if we get all we wanted and more it *still* isn't what we were hoping for.

In this story in the Bible we see a woman who had reached out to all types of people and sought all types of answers for her condition. We're not sure what caused her bleeding or even all that she had tried—but she kept getting the same dead-end results. Have you ever felt that way? When you finally do get your hands on what you were reaching for it doesn't really meet the need?

- If you had to take an honest look at your life right now, what would you say you're reaching for?
- Can you name some things you reached for in the past that left you less than satisfied?

b. What are you expecting?

Ever put on an old coat and, somewhere in your day, stick your hand in the coat pocket to get your keys and instead you pull out a dollar or even a five-dollar bill? Surprises like that are nice, aren't they? But life's usually not like that; we usually know what we can expect when we reach in that pocket. We all seem to be reaching for something—but the question is: What are we expecting to get?

If you're reaching for money, your phone, a new iPod, or even a job, what are you expecting to get with that item? You might say, "Isn't it obvious?" With everything we reach for in life we have some type of expectation, whether realistic or not. Is your Christian life what you expected it to be? Are you getting what you were hoping for? Every person who comes to Christ has different expectations. Some want their pain gone, others want a question answered, and still others are looking to fill a deep void in their heart.

Now here's the point: What are you expecting in your walk with God? You have to believe that the twelve apostles, when they first began to follow Christ, had totally different expectations from that moment to when he ascended into heaven a few years later. Their expectations changed over time as they got closer to Christ and to his mission.

How might your expectations change as you get closer to Christ in your walk with him? Maybe as you look back over the time you've been a Christian, you can already see how your expectations have changed.

God's Word speaks directly to what we can expect when we follow Christ—we just need to dig to find what those expectations should be, and we need hearts a little more like the woman in this story.

BURST:

BRANDED:

2. Touch Changes Things

a. When you're desperate

Let's take a closer look at this woman who sought out Jesus. It's fair to say she's on a mission. She wants to be healed. She has a problem that no one has been able to solve up to this point, and she hopes that a simple touch will change everything. In short, she is desperate.

Everyone in this room has at one time or another touched something hot. Whether you knew it was hot or not, you *really* knew once you touched it. And it changed you. You might have gotten a scar or a blister or even a bad dream out of it, but you came away changed. We touch things every day that change us. We touch video games, music, friends, schoolwork, the Bible, computers—the list goes on and on. But think about this: How are those things changing you? Believe it or not, everything you touch rubs off on you. Is it rubbing off for good or for bad?

BURST:

BRANDED:

b. What are you touching?

What would happen if you made a point to touch Jesus every day in your daily routine? You may not see a big change immediately but over time your life will begin to look different—just as it surely looked different for that woman.

It's as simple—and as challenging—as doing it every day for just a few minutes each day. A few verses, a few minutes in meditation on what you read, and a few minutes in prayer—and over time what you are touching *will* change you.

It's been said that who you are in ten years will be a direct result of what you're taking in and who you're hanging around with today. So who are you spending your time with and what are you taking in?

FOR DISCUSSION:

- Have you ever touched something that burned you—not in the physical sense, but in the spiritual sense?
- Have you ever touched something—or been touched by someone's life—that left you changed for the better?
- What are ways you can touch Jesus each day to get closer to him?
- How can we help each other get in touch with Jesus each day and each week?

3. He Knows

a. Effort rewarded

If you've ever been on a road trip with your family and your family had young kids you *know* you heard someone yell, at some point, "He's touching me!" The parents are desperately trying to keep the kids calm, but it soon becomes a game in which one of them has to try to catch the perpetrator. If it goes on long enough, you'll hear the driver yell, "Don't make me pull this car over!"

But there's no guessing with Jesus. He knows who touched him. In fact, Jesus knows the people who are just *reaching* for him.

In his encounter with this woman, Jesus is surrounded by hundreds of people. Amazingly, he stops and asks the question, "Who touched me?" There were so many pressing against him on all sides—what made the difference, what made him stop? This woman was touching Jesus and *expecting something in return.* Her faith made it impossible for her not to receive notice from Jesus. Even in today's world, with all the busyness, God knows when someone is in need, when someone is trying to touch him—he notices. This woman fought through the crowd and wrestled her way near Jesus' presence.

This is what we must do daily. You may have to wrestle through your day, your problems, and your pressures to touch God, but if you do, he will know you're trying and you will be changed because of the effort.

BURST:

BRANDED:

b. Hundreds didn't

There are many out there who claim to be Christians. There are many, even, who seem to do all the right things. But many of these same people completely miss the point of who Jesus is. The people who surrounded Jesus and all but smothered his disciples missed the point of his being there. They could have touched Jesus with more than their hands. They could have touched him with their hearts or turned to him with the faith that he could touch areas of their lives in which they needed help. But only the woman seemed to really *touch* him.

Many people have areas of their lives they wish God would touch. Are you one of the desperate ones who are ready to fight through the crowd of distractions and grab hold of him?

Wrap It Up

Is Jesus asking you, "Did you touch me?" Have you gone after it, given him the opportunity to ask you that question?

What are the pressures of each day or week you need to press through in order to touch Jesus? Do you ever feel like the crowd is closing in and you may not reach him? Keep fighting for that touch; he knows you are there. He is ready to connect.

ALTERED

What's needed: A wooden *cross on a table or floor stand* (many churches have them and one can be borrowed if yours doesn't); a *cloth*; some *soft mood music or soft worship music* can help with this activity

At the end of the message ask students to take a stand to increase their "touch time" with their heavenly Father. Invite them to come up front, where you have draped a cloth over the cross. As they approach, have them hold the cloth and say a short prayer. Don't rush this; allow your students time to pray.

Playing some soft music, as noted above, gives this activity a nice touch.

If you have a larger group, ask two to four students to pray at the cross at the same time.

End the night with group prayer.

A.S.K.
(ASK, SEEK, KNOCK)

WHAT IT'S ALL ABOUT

God rewards persistence in prayer; this is a clear teaching of Jesus. We must learn how to push through in a world that expects life to be effortless and easy and, if not, gives up easily when it is not.

Prayer is hard work. Youth pastors and leaders, you get a chance to set the pace for students to **A**sk, **S**eek, and **K**nock!

Get It Started

What's needed: A single *feather* (once again, you are welcome!)

Ever play bloody knuckles? The point is to get the other person to give up before you do. You inflict pain after the flip of a quarter determines who gets whacked on the knuckles (usually with a deck of cards) . . . But no, do *NOT* play bloody knuckles! Not a good idea to try that one in youth group! (We repeat: Do not . . .)

OK, so that's straight. You're going to try this game instead. It has the same end goal and is more fun anyway: Fluffy Giggles. What, you say? Get students to volunteer in pairs and see if one friend can make the other laugh by using a feather to tickle them in different places. Before starting, one of them has to take off his or her shoes and socks, exposing their feet; then have them roll up their sleeves if they're wearing long sleeves.

Have the other friend use that little feather on the neck, the face, the arms (biceps, forearms, wrist, or hand), and the tops and then bottoms of the feet if all else fails. (Make sure you keep the tickling to only those areas. If someone makes it through all areas—more power to them!)

Did we mention that people most likely will give in to the giggles? See who can get tickled in the most places before the laughter breaks out.

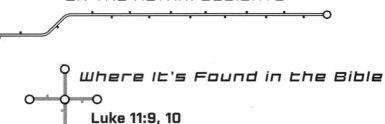

Where It's Found in the Bible

Luke 11:9, 10

If you have time, read Luke 11:1-8 as well; it has more great lessons on prayer.

"So I say to you: Ask and it will be given to you; seek and you will find; knock and the door will be opened to you. For everyone who asks receives; he who seeks finds; and to him who knocks, the door will be opened."

1. Where Are My Keys?

a. He said ASK

Have you ever felt this? There you are again, searching, looking, hoping, and wondering as the clock goes tick, tick, tick . . . You look in your pants pocket, then the pants you wore yesterday, and then the pants you wore last week. You look under the table, on the table, and around the table. You look by the phone, by the door, and in the car. When you're done you start the whole process over again as if your keys will magically appear.

Now you start to ask everyone in the house: "Have you seen my keys?" "Mom, have you seen my keys?" "Dad, have you seen my keys?" "Hey little squirt, have you seen my keys?" "Hey dog: seen my keys?" Yes, you're now asking your dog!

We can all relate to the lost keys syndrome. Whether it's your car keys, your wallet, your phone, or MP3 player, we all can relate to searching for something in a panic. And why does it always happen when we're in a hurry and have to be somewhere? If you're like most people, you won't give up until you find them. Even if you have to come back later you keep looking, searching, praying, and asking everyone—until you find those keys.

BURST:

BRANDED:

b. Why settle for less?

Have you ever wondered what it would be like to have a prayer life in which you search as hard on your knees as you do for lost things in your life? What would your life look like with that kind of prayer life? Let's go back to the lost keys for a minute. Have you ever looked everywhere and wasted hours and then just happened to ask your mom where your keys are and she says . . . "Yeah, matter of fact, they're in the fridge, right where you left them." How much time you would have saved had you asked earlier!—or just decided to have a soda.

Many times we go through life and settle for less than we should and expect less than we should just because we don't—or won't—take the time to ask. Jesus gives us a simple yet powerful key to prayer in these verses. We must ask, seek, and knock. Yes, the easy way to remember it is A-S-K: ASK. So the key is asking.

Many times we ask and don't get what we're looking for and then we give up. We assume God isn't listening, but maybe it's that we're the ones not listening. God wants us to continue asking because it helps us in a few ways. First, if we ask and don't get our prayers answered—but we keep asking—it may begin to change how and what we ask for. The more we pray the more his voice shapes what we're asking for. We may be asking for a date with the hot girl in school and he may not seem to answer at first—or ever! But as we pray we get in tune with his voice and we may hear him say that a date with the hot girl will not meet the need we feel inside. And maybe, even, *you* are not what that young lady needs in her life. As we ask he changes our requests so that we do get what we need and not just what we want.

FOR DISCUSSION WITH YOUR GROUP:

- Have you ever prayed for something that you later found out would not have been a good thing if you had received it? Share that story.
- Have you ever had God refine what you were looking for as a result of praying?

c. Persist at persisting

One of the greatest speeches given in modern times also was one of the simplest. In October 1941 Winston Churchill, prime minister of England, spoke to a group of students. His country's war against Hitler and Germany was getting more difficult and more intense with every month that went by. He said other things that day, but these words were the centerpiece: "Never give in, never give in, never, never, never, never—in nothing, great or small, large or petty—never give in except to convictions of honour and good sense."[1] Seems simple enough, but how many of us live by those words?

In the few short verses in our Luke 11 passage Jesus basically said the same thing. Or, we should say, Churchill basically said what Jesus first said. Jesus says to ask, seek, and knock . . . continually . . . until we get our answer.

So how much are you willing to search? As much as you would if you lost your keys, your wallet, or your phone? The truth for too many people is that they will search longer for these other items than they will for an answer to prayer—and that is why many people are stuck where they are in life.

2. Knock Knock . . .

a. Who's there?

The word here for *knock* actually means "rap"—as in a loud, sharp knocking, a knocking that is continual and purposeful. Here is another insight into what God wants us to do in prayer. There must be an urgency to our prayers that makes us think through our time with him. We have to pray about more than just everyday needs; we pray about what's most important to our lives. When you're really seeking God over the big things in life (temptation, attitude, lust, greed, lack of faith) there's an urgency, much like when you're rapping on a door trying to get in before an approaching dog takes a big bite out of your backside. One knock won't cut it. You knock and knock and knock and knock until your knuckles are bloody. You have to have someone answer that door; your life depends on it. That's the type of urgency that will bring your prayers to life.

b. You can't earn it

Prayer can seem like work. But this doesn't mean that if you pray long enough or hard enough you earn it. If we put all these pieces together we see that it's not *hard* work but the *kind* of work that does more than just give us the answers you're looking for; it changes us. And that is the most important thing in life. When you ask God for answers you're admitting your dependence on him. When you seek him you're showing your heart's motive and when you knock—really *knock*—you're assured that you are praying for the most important things in your life.

If you search for answers like this with as much intensity as you look for the lost items in your life, you'll be amazed at the transformation you begin to make. Let the lost things in your life be a reminder of how your time with God should be. Don't go another week searching for things more than you search for God.

BURST:

BRANDED:

3. A.S.K.

a. Ask

So what was the last thing you really wanted? You thought about it all the time and you asked everyone how to get it. You *schemed* about how to get it. Now think about that item compared to . . . what is it that you really want to ask God for the most? What are those eternal desires that you have to have answers to? Now is the time to get serious about them and go after God with your requests. Don't just ask—ask with urgency. And God has said it will be given to you.

FOR DISCUSSION:

- What is the one thing that you really desire from God, the one thing you want to start asking for today? (Note to leaders: don't force sharing. Students should share only if they wish.)

b. Seek

How will you search? What's the plan that you've come up with to find what it is you're looking for? When will you pray and how will you pray and how long will you pray? What will you do to keep distractions from your pursuit? We all need a plan to seek him or our human nature will lead us to give up sooner or later. Remember: as soon as you start to pray for what is most important it seems as though the whole world is trying to keep you from it. But God promises that he who seeks will find.

FOR DISCUSSION:

- What plan can you go after, starting today, to really seek God?

c. Knock

A "to-do" list is necessary for many people to keep their lives in order. And really, you need one in your prayer life to keep that part of your life in order. What is on your prayer to-do list? What does God want on your list? What are those things that are so urgent that you must have an answer to them? Make sure you don't just look at the need—but also the reason it is a need in your life. Then knock—hard, over and over—knowing that God is behind that door and has said he will answer.

FOR DISCUSSION:

- What items can you share that will be on your prayer list?

Wrap It Up

What are you ready to ask God for—with urgency? What plans will you put in place to really seek him—to not be satisfied, to make sure you overcome the distractions, until you find him? What will be on your to-do list so that you're sure you're knocking with the urgency that you must have an answer?

ALTERED

What's needed: *boxes of Band-Aids; pens*

Have boxes of Band-Aids available at the altar area. Invite students to take three Band-Aids and spell out A-S-K, putting one letter on each Band-Aid. They'll then put the adhesives on a notebook that they often use, or the front of their Bibles, or inside their locker at school, or in some other place of their choice. They might place the letters on an arm or across the back of their hand. These are a great personal reminder in school, or in front of others, of the A-S-K message.

End the night with prayer.

WHAT'S IT GOING TO COST?
(BOUGHT AT A PRICE)

WHAT IT'S ALL ABOUT

Everyone wants to know the bottom line. It's simply this: "What's it going to cost?" We ask that question every day in hundreds of ways, big and small. What we want, what we wear, where we go—even who we talk to and hang out with. All of these have a cost. What's it going to cost me if I make that decision? What's it going to cost me if I take my youth group on that trip? And on and on.

What's the price that God paid for each of us? And what will it cost us to serve him? That's what this meeting is about.

Get It Started

What's needed: Surf the Internet and find *photos or advertisements for outrageous clothes* that cost unbelievable amounts of money. Look for shoes, jewelry, dresses, hairstyles, even a purse or two. Men's suits, men's shoes, whatever works. Capture the pictures and *put them into a PowerPoint show* for your students.

Have students guess the value of each item. Don't be afraid to throw the tacky, bargain basement item in with the ridiculously expensive. This keeps it interesting!

Have small prizes for the winners. Or, after some buildup, make the prizes color prints of the expensive items.

Options: Working in small groups, have your students add up how much money they estimate that they or their parents spent on what they're wearing at this meeting. Have them total up clothes, perfume, jewelry, shoes—whatever they're wearing that cost money! Let students in other groups guess the totals and see which group comes closest.

More options: Have the guys go against the girls in either of the above options.

Where It's Found in the Bible

1 Corinthians 6:20

You were bought at a price. Therefore honor God with your body.

YOUTH TALK OUTLINE

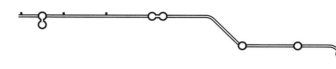

1. What's It Going to Cost?

a. And if you act now . . .

Have you ever been up late at night, just hanging with a friend, and you start surfing TV channels? Who hasn't, right? So you stumble on an advertisement for the "handy dandy super cereal box top opener 5000!" The announcer quickly whips you into a frenzy; he's saying this is . . . one . . . incredible . . . deal. And you're starting to believe him! You say to yourself, *I'll be able to open cereal box tops faster than any of my friends! Man, they'll be jealous! We've got to get this thing for our house!* All you need to know is how much it costs! You're saying to the TV, "I'm ready . . . just tell me!" But every time they're about to tell you they throw something else in the deal. You hear the words, "And if you act *now* . . . You'll get the travel version and a free spoon!" The whole time you just keep asking, "OK, but how much is it going to cost?!?"

But there's a question far better than that one. How much did it cost God to save us from our sins? Imagine if that question suddenly popped on the screen while you were watching that ad, or during the game tonight, or during your favorite show, or in the middle of a movie—what would be your first thought? Maybe you'd quickly blurt out, in a religious sort of way: "Jesus." But what it really cost was someone's life, their blood, their final breath. And not just anyone's life—a sinless one. God was willing to do this with one man's life in order to pay the full price for my sin and yours.

BURST:

BRANDED:

b. Cheap sunglasses

Some people make a habit of littering sunglasses all over the United States. They go on trips and lose two or three pair; they go through about eight pair, it seems, every year. Maybe you're one of those people. So then imagine that one day your mom or grandmother decides to buy you one very expensive pair of designer sunglasses. You immediately panic: *What will I tell her when I lose them?* You know it will just be a matter of time before you set that $200 pair of glasses down in a restaurant and walk away—and then what? Will you lie and tell her you gave them to an organization that collects sunglasses for the blind?

But then you find a funny thing happening with that particular pair of glasses— you never lose them! So why do the things like this in life, the things that we know are worth more, seem to last? Because we know what they cost and we live with the knowledge of the price paid for them. We seem to understand that it's OK to lose a pair of $20 glasses but it's not OK to lose a $200 pair. We find ourselves constantly watching over that kind of purchase like a hawk.

1 Corinthians 6:20 says that we were "bought at a price." But unless we know

what that price is we may not live accordingly. This could be a little like having a pair of sunglasses that we thought were worth $25 only to find out after we lost them that they were actually $2,500 glasses. It's the same in our daily walk with God. We must know and continually remind ourselves of the price that was paid for us to live free from sin and a life of guilt. How sad and disrespectful to God and his Son to treat our life like . . . a pair of cheap sunglasses.

2. How Much?

a. Free—at a cost

What's it going to cost me to serve God? It's been said that salvation costs us nothing, but living for God costs us everything.

Have you ever watched those antique shows on TV? They can be kind of fascinating—not so much because of the things that people bring in to be appraised but because of the people themselves. Ask yourself: Who in their right mind would travel hours in a car, spend all that gas money, pay for a hotel, stand in line until their legs are numb—and all this to show off an old wooden spoon! Then, to top it off, the expert says, "Yes, it is in fact an antique, and it's worth nearly $100!" You think, *Was it really worth it for that person?*

We may "know" how much God paid for our sins, but do we understand the real cost—both for God and for us? Think about that previous statement: "Salvation costs you nothing, but to live for God costs you everything." It's like winning a brand new Corvette—let's say that happens sometime in the next ten years. You think it's free—and it is—but you quickly realize there is a price to pay for a free Corvette. You have to pay state taxes, licensing, title, insurance, and then maybe even a place to store it during the winter months. And let's not forget the premium gas to run that baby. So was it free? Yes! Did it cost you? Yes! Is salvation free? Yes! Does serving God cost us? Yes!

[Note: James 2 makes a great further study on this topic.]

FOR DISCUSSION WITH YOUR GROUP:

- Can you think of something that you thought was free but later found out was going to cost you something—maybe even a lot?
- Think about Jesus on the cross: Why is it easy to see that as free, and not see the real price that was paid?

b. What are you willing to pay?

So there is a cost, there is a price, for almost everything. There definitely was for

Jesus hanging on the cross. So now we have to ask ourselves, *How will I pay and how much will I pay?* Do you remember what the verse in 1 Corinthians 6 said? "You were bought at a price—therefore, honor God . . . "

The cost is to honor our God with our entire selves! What does it mean to honor God? Simply put, it means to make God look good—no, awesome!—by what we think, say, do, act. By how we live.

Our price is to honor the Father day in and day out. The good news is that God already has said that he will give us the power to do this, through his Holy Spirit.

BURST:

BRANDED:

3. What's the True Value?

a. God is worth it

Go into a store and you'll usually find two different mind-sets among shoppers. The first: How does it look? Whether you're looking for clothes, shoes, belts, fashion, hair, or makeup, you want to know how it will look. The other mind-set: How does it work—or even, *does* it work? Men go into a hardware store looking at power tools and they usually want to know: Does it work? Not, how does it look? Can you imagine going into a hardware store and asking where they've got the pink hammers? Or purchasing a pair of Italian pumps and asking how well the heel can hammer nails. The Bible tells us that we were created for good works, not good looks. Ephesians 2:10 says, "We are God's workmanship, created in Christ Jesus to do good works, which God prepared in advance for us to do." Think of what that means! We're to honor God with our works, not our looks. We make God look good by working for him. He set up awesome things for you—especially, *only* you—to do for him.

FOR DISCUSSION:

- How can we approach living for God so that we're thinking of how we will work for him, not what we look like while working for him?

b. You are worth it

OK, so many of you tonight are worth a few hundred dollars just in what you're wearing on your bodies! But don't be fooled—you're worth far more than that and for way more important reasons. With God's Spirit in you and the gifts he has given you, you're worth beyond what you can imagine. And he's enabled you to honor him, in return, with your whole being.

BURST:

BRANDED:

Wrap It Up

We're going to ask you to take time to come forward and pray and ask God to help you honor him and the price he paid. When you're finished praying, take one of the dollar bills that are up front and be willing to put one of your own one-dollar bills with it. Then you're going to ask God how you can use this small amount to honor him this week. All you need to be willing to do is honor him in whatever way he asks you.

Remember, God has already planned good works for you—large and small—so he already knows the many ways you can serve him.

ALTERED

What's needed: *A dollar bill for as many students* as will be in attendance; *write 1 Corinthians 6:20 on a small sheet of paper and paper-clip to each dollar*

Give each student a dollar and challenge them to glorify God that day or the next, at the latest, with the dollar given them and just one of their own dollars that they'll add to it.

Paper-clip the 1 Corinthians 6:20 verse onto each bill that you lay up front at the altar area.

Here are some simple ideas to show how much can be done (for God), even with little:
• Buy someone's bus fare
• Buy someone a coffee or something to eat
• Buy an encouraging card to give to a struggling friend or two (there are now lots of 99-cent card racks out there)
• Buy a student ticket to one of the high school games for a student who doesn't have the money or doesn't get to go to many games
• Buy something from the vending machine for a friend at school
• Buy something for the person who often sits alone at lunch; invite that person to sit with you

Ministry idea: During next week's meeting, have your students share testimonies of how they honored God with their gift.

End the night with prayer.

SOMETHING'S IN THE WATER! (THE POWER OF SERVING)

WHAT IT'S ALL ABOUT

What does it mean to serve? Sweat? Blood? Tears? Those are all noble, but sometimes the simple actions can mean just as much. Jesus said that serving can be as simple as a cup of cold water.

Thinking big is great, but it's easy for students—and leaders, too—to get overwhelmed with where to start to change our world. You'll use this meeting to give your students a lesson on serving, starting with baby steps. You'll challenge them to serve a cup of cold water in the name of Christ.

Get It Started

What's needed: A *long table*, lots of *Styrofoam cups filled about three-fourths full with water*, *a large tarp* to place under the table, and you'll probably want *a mop*

You may have seen some of those cup-stacking competitions where kids stack cups at insane speeds. They're good—but could they do it with cups full of water?

Set up a table with a big tarp underneath and give your students a chance to stack cups of water as high as they can—pyramid form is usually best, but maybe you have something else in mind or maybe your students do.

They can do this competition individually or in teams. Find out who has the steadiest hand. (Go for height and not necessarily speed.) It's guaranteed a mess will be made; outside may be the best place for this if the weather is nice. If not, be prepared to spend at least a little time with the mop!

Where It's Found in the Bible

Matthew 10:42

"And if anyone gives even a cup of cold water to one of these little ones because he is my disciple, I tell you the truth, he will certainly not lose his reward."

YOUTH TALK OUTLINE

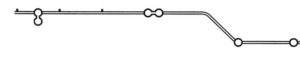

1. It's Just Water

   a. It's the little things

We all have needs and desires in life, but many times it's when the most simple of our desires is not met that we really feel it. Take, for instance, quenching your thirst. You probably don't think about your thirst much and you probably don't have meeting that need on your to-do list for today. But it is a need and it's even one that can drive you mad—or kill you—if you can't fill it for too long of a time. We've all been so thirsty that our throat is thick with spit and we start to dream of ice-cold liquid, of any sort, pouring down our throats. We wonder why we left the house without a water bottle. We think: *Make it lemonade, Gatorade, or even mustard-ade—just make it cold and make it fast!* When someone finally comes along with an ice-cold bottle of water we're so thankful we're ready to name our firstborn child after them.

If you're not thirsty it may not seem like a big deal to give a bottle of water to someone. But if you're on the receiving end of that need it feels like life or death.

<u>Do you think that, at times as Christians, we forget what it's like to be truly thirsty, to be looking for that one thing in life that will quench our spiritual thirst?</u> It's good to remember that we were once thirsty and that there are others around us who still have plenty of thirst. It hurts to think that we can walk around with the Spirit of God flowing through us and yet keep that Spirit bottled up and to ourselves.

How many people do we walk past on a daily basis who are spiritually dry and thirsty inside? What if they knew that we had the water of life? In fact, Jesus does! In John 7:37, Jesus told a large crowd of people, "If anyone is thirsty, let him come to me and drink."

Who would refuse a cup of cold water if they were truly thirsty?

BURST:

BRANDED:

b. It has to be cold

Here are some things that most people hate: stale popcorn, flat pop, brown apples, wilted lettuce, warm water. These are always worse when you expect them to be fresh or cold—whichever applies—and they're just the opposite. There's just something inside of us that refuses to settle for cheap substitutes! Don't get it wrong: If you're thirsty and trapped in the desert, you'll drink hot water as long as it's liquid. But when it's cold, icy, and the bottle is dripping with condensation, it's far better. Some things are just better cold—water is one of them.

Why did Jesus point to a cup of cold water as an appropriate gift for his "little ones," for those following him? The answer is more simple than we might think: It was hard to get a simple cup of cold water back in Christ's day. Think about it: They couldn't just walk up to the faucet or open the refrigerator and pull out cold water. There were no soft drink machines. To get cold water you had to pull a bag or bucket from a well, put the water in a clay pot, and keep that pot in a cool place—and then you had to transport it as quickly as possible to the person you were trying to bless. Put another way, you had to really think about it and plan it; this was not just something you easily whipped up.

The best ways to serve are when it's the right thing at the right time for the right person—this takes planning.

FOR DISCUSSION WITH YOUR GROUP:

- How can you serve someone in your life in the next few days? How will you think through what you're going to do?

2. The Little Things Make All the Difference

a. Serve the "little ones"

Too many times we get caught up in all the huge things that seem to need attention or all the big needs that seem to be crying out for help. In other words, we can focus all our time and energy on the squeaky wheels around us. It's easy to overlook those who are out of the way, hidden behind all the busyness, or not in the public eye. Look again at the passage: Jesus specifically says we are to help "the little ones"—and he's not necessarily talking about children (though we should serve and bless them also). We know this because he goes on to say those he's talking about are his disciples, a word that essentially means "follower" and is a synonym for a true Christian. Jesus calls us to serve those who get looked down on as the little people. Yes, there are times to get involved in the big problems of life, but it's more practical to get involved in the little things day after day.

Think about it for a second: When most people look to serve, they look to serve the major cause, the superstar, the person who will bring them attention. This is why Christ's words are so powerful today. There are great and grand causes out there and we can get pulled in multiple directions by all these things. But what if we simply sought to serve those who don't get any headlines? What if we made it a priority to serve the hurting people in little ways? God says this will have a huge impact on them and on us.

BURST:

BRANDED:

b. The difference a cup of water makes

Imagine if Jesus had said, "Anyone who gives a cup of gold to these little ones . . . " Now *that*, we might say, would be service. But no—the power behind Jesus' words is the simplicity of the action he calls us to.

Take your running shoes for example. What cool shoelaces, right? Shoelaces are usually not the focus of anyone's shoes; no one goes out and says, "Look at those laces! I have to buy those right now!" You don't call your friend and tell him or her about the cool new shoelaces you bought—it's always about the shoes. Yet as insignificant as the laces might seem, try to play basketball or soccer or any other game without them. You quickly find out how important shoelaces are! All of a sudden your $175 kicks are no better than the $45 ones—even worse, if you don't have those laces. You would give your new shoes for any other pair of shoes in the middle of a big game—especially if they had laces.

If we're open, and listening, to God's leading we can, day in and day out, do the simple things that make a big difference in his kingdom.

Maybe our Christian example suffers not because we ignore the big but because we ignore the little. How much might it mean to mow a neighbor's lawn, drive the loner student to school, or say hi to the new kid at school? What might it mean to put your arm around your mom or dad and tell them you love them? Or encourage the girl sitting next to you in class? What might it mean to invite the kid to the party who no one spends time with—and actually spend time with him?

All are little cups of water that will make a big splash!

FOR DISCUSSION:

- What stops us from reaching out to the "little ones?" Why are we hesitant to make the first steps?
- Why is there so much power in what Jesus is saying? How can we help each other obey Christ in this command?

3. 'Will Surely Not Lose His Reward . . .'

a. Surprise inside!

Who doesn't love a prize? Probably all of us, as kids, loved the cereal that came with the prizes inside. You know the routine: you get up early, get out a cookie sheet or bowl, open the box and pour all the cereal out onto the sheet or bowl, and shuffle through all that sugary cereal until you find the prize! Then you shovel it all back in the box and put the cereal back in the cupboard and not even eat any of it. You just want the prize! And even "big kids" still do this today since they started putting Guitar Hero stuff in cereal boxes!

We don't like to talk about "prizes" when it comes to serving Jesus and others—but there are prizes. Jesus says that if we serve the least, the forgotten, the little ones, we will surely get our reward. This isn't to say we serve just to get some sort of prize, or reward, but one thing we can see in life: those who serve others always seem to be the happiest, the most joyful, the most content. God wants us to live that kind of life! He blesses those who bless others; it's that simple.

BURST:

BRANDED:

b. Take the plunge

"The proof is in the pudding." Growing up, did you ever hear that silly saying? Have you ever been eating some pudding and found proof in it? Well, Jesus says that the proof of your discipleship is in the water. If you are truly a disciple then you will seek to serve.

Jesus' encouragement is to step up and serve "the least of these"—as he put it in a similar passage in Matthew 25—with a cup of cold water.

Is God putting someone on your heart today who you can begin to reach out to this week?

Wrap It Up

Who might be the last, or least, person you'd think of serving? How might you reach out to them and allow yourself to be used by God? It may seem simple, but as you take this Altar challenge pray about who you're supposed to give your water to—and believe that even though it's a small thing, God will bless them and reward you.

ALTERED

What's needed: *Bottles of water,* one for as many students as will be in attendance

Invite your students to come up front and take a bottle of water from the altar area. Ask them to give it to someone this week with a note, sharing their faith.

Stress that the water may indeed bless someone, but the bottles are mostly meant as a symbol of a serving lifestyle. Challenge your students to follow the lesson's main points and think of small ways they can serve—especially the "little ones"—this week.

End the night with prayer.

THE ROCK
(A COVENANT WITH GOD)

WHAT IT'S ALL ABOUT

Being a Christian is not a solo act! It's a group thing! This meeting is about getting all of your students involved in the cause of taking a stand as one body. You'll teach them the importance of keeping each other accountable.

If you choose the ministry option at the end of this session, you'll also leave a visible sign, placed in the church entryway, for all to see.

For this meeting: Before any students arrive, place a *large stone* up front, or in the middle of the youth room. Students will be asking about it—but hold them off, referring to the talk to come.

Get It Started

What's needed: Line up *a number of songs* from Christian musicians: whether David Crowder, Jeremy Camp, Casting Crowns, Jaci Velasquez—whoever your students listen to

This one's simple: Name That Rock. Take a minute and play Name That Tune with some of the most popular Christian rock tunes. Play just a few seconds of each song and see who knows their music! Giving away CDs to the fastest is a great way to make it fun.

Options: Maybe throw in a few gospel choir tunes, or Elvis, or the Rolling Stones, or some ancient Jackson 5, just for sheer confusion. Maybe a few Weird Al Yankovic songs for absolutely no reason!

Where It's Found in the Bible

Joshua 24:24-27

And the people said to Joshua, "We will serve the Lord our God and obey him."
On that day Joshua made a covenant for the people, and there at Shechem he drew up for them decrees and laws. And Joshua recorded these things in the Book of the Law of God. Then he took a large stone and set it up there under the oak near the holy place of the Lord.

"See!" he said to all the people. "This stone will be a witness against us. It has heard all the words the Lord has said to us. It will be a witness against you if you are untrue to your God."

YOUTH TALK OUTLINE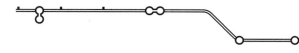

1. Promises, Promises

a. Heard it a thousand times before

Have you ever felt this way? "Is there anyone I can believe when they say, 'I promise'"? Maybe you've heard absurd stories about monkeys flying in pink swimsuits or creatures from Mars and your friend wants you to believe them so badly that they utter those well-known words: "I promise." Or maybe you're checking out at the grocery store and find yourself looking at a magazine that says Elvis was seen eating at a McDonald's and you say, "Impossible! Everyone knows Elvis liked Burger King more!" Here's the thing: Promises are often empty, especially when broken by the one giving them.

In this story in Israel's history, very near the end of Joshua's life, God's leader faces the reality that the Israelites have made many promises about serving God. Their actions, however, often spoke differently than what their promises promised! In fact, Joshua gave them a short history lesson, just before this talk, about all the times they had blown it.

Maybe you could compare those to the times when you told your parents you would get that lawn mowed or you'd clean your room and . . . you promise. Then your Mom pulls out of her air-tight memory all the times you promised and didn't follow through. All you can say is, "Uhhh, yeah, about that . . . "

This is where the nation of Israel finds itself. This is where Joshua finds the people: Empty promises. One after another. Joshua has heard this too many times. "We will serve the Lord our God." He decided that it's time for the Israelites to live up to their words.

BURST:

BRANDED:

b. Set up to be set apart

When you finally get busted for not mowing that lawn or not cleaning your room you may, in frustration, tell your mom that you wanted to, really, you did. So what happened? Things got in the way and your girlfriend called and there was a show on TV and the sky was blue and . . . We all mean well but many times we just don't get it done. Or maybe you're in your room and you hear your parents' car drive up and . . . *"Ding!"* You realize you haven't cleaned your room yet and you kick it into hyperdrive—shoveling clothes into your closet along with candy wrappers, dirty dishes, and a couple of fast food bags.

But what if your parents asked if you were going to clean your room and you promised and then they said, "OK, but are you willing to bet your plans with your friends for tonight on it?" Now you have to put your money where your mouth is. Are you willing to commit to the deal?

In this story in the Bible, Joshua calls the Israelites to a higher standard by saying they must make a covenant. To make a covenant with God is to provide a sign to others, and to yourself, that you are choosing to be separated for God and set apart from others. The word itself means a "formal, solemn, and binding agreement." Joshua challenges the people to serve God—and they agree. The only thing is, they soon find out that Joshua is serious about their decision. So serious that he calls them to accountability.

FOR DISCUSSION WITH YOUR GROUP:

- What's one of the biggest promises you've ever made with another person—a friend, parent, another relative, teacher, or coach?
- Can you see a value in making a solemn promise to God? What would it be; why would someone do that?

2. It's in the Book

a. Write it down

Some people love to-do lists. They have to-do lists under their to-do lists. Sometimes the only way to know that you'll remember to get something done is to make a list. Ever go to the store for your mom and once you're there you forget what she wanted? You could have written it down, but instead you come home with chips, milk, batteries, and a bag of marshmallows. All she wanted was sugar and butter.

It may seem like the big things should be easier to remember, but not even the Israelites could remember the important things without writing them down. Joshua records all that they promised to do. Now you know it's serious!

Ever see a cop at an accident scene with his little notepad? He is taking down what everyone saw. He wants all the details so when people show up in court he can recount all that was said and hold them to their stories.

Joshua was doing a very similar same thing to what that cop does. He was writing down the details so the people would always remember.

THE ROCK (A COVENANT WITH GOD)

- Why is it easy to choose to live for God one day—and then the next we completely forget the decision we made?
- Would it help to write our decisions down and check in with them every day, or at least a few times a week? What other ways can we remind ourselves each day of the commitment we made to Christ?

b. Witness protection

Have you ever done something so stupid that you just couldn't believe it, and worse yet, there were people there to witness it? You wish no one would have seen you fall off that chair into the fish tank while choking on your popsicle, but your friends were right there when it happened. The next day at school people are whispering and laughing and it's all they seem to be talking about. So the embarrassment is yours to carry around and because just a few people saw it now everyone knows. That's the power of someone witnessing something. On a more serious note, witnesses are the key to solving any crime and many times they make or break the case against a person.

It's the same in living for Christ. Witnesses are needed—but this time in a positive way, big time! We can call them witnesses, but really, they're accountability partners. They keep us towing the line and when we want to give up they keep us on track. It would be so cool to have someone wake us up every morning and remind us of our decision to follow Christ, right? But most of us don't have the luxury of having that person—and Mom doesn't count. So we need witnesses; we need partners in the faith.

BURST:

BRANDED:

3. Rock On

a. God and some pretty important rocks

Ever know someone who collects rocks? They come in all colors and shapes and textures and have names like malachite-cuprite. Try saying that five times fast!

Rocks and stones—not such a big deal, right? But there are some very important rocks and stones in the Bible. Here are just a few:

- there's the stone that David cut down Goliath with
- you've got the stone "the builders rejected" that Jesus talked about in referring to people rejecting him
- the stone that was rolled away from the tomb—that could be the most famous stone in history!
- and the stone that Joshua set up as a witness

Why was Joshua's stone so special? Well, it was more than just another rock. It was a symbol of what had just taken place between the nation of Israel and Joshua. This rock was set up next to an altar—"the holy place of the Lord," the passage says—and it was to serve as a witness to the words spoken by the people. It would be a sign of all that they had said and done.

Imagine waking up every day and having a big rock on your bed as a reminder of something! You'd feel that thing; it would be easy to remember something starting your day that way! And when your friends walked into your room and saw that rock on your covers, you know they'd ask about it.

We don't need a rock on our beds but we *do* need something to continually reaffirm our decisions and remind us daily to continue to live for God.

BURST:

BRANDED:

b. Be true to your word

Ever hear your voice played back on a recording? You think, *I can't believe I sound that weird!* What if we could play back all the times we made promises to God? That might be a little more than we're comfortable with, but maybe that should be the point! And that was the point with Joshua's large rock. It was to be seen by the people every day—by their kids, their grandkids, and many generations after them. It would forever be a reminder of what was said on that day. That rock was their recording—one they could never erase.

The point of this rock is that it worked! When we read the rest of the chapter we see that this generation did live for God—for years and years after this time. "Israel served the Lord throughout the lifetime of Joshua and of the elders who outlived him" [Joshua 24:31]. This stone worked! It was a daily reminder to the Israelites.

Wrap It Up

We need daily reminders in our lives. We need simple yet effective ways to keep us reflecting on our daily decisions and choices. Are you ready to rock your world for Christ? A simple reminder at the end of this meeting will help.

ALTERED

What's needed: The *large stone* that you placed in the youth room before the message; a number of *wide-tip markers of different colors*

Now come back to the rock that's been in the room for the entire message. Tell your students that this rock—like Joshua's rock—has heard everything said at this meeting. It will be a witness to these words. Invite your students to come up front and sign it.

Ministry idea: If possible, and if the church staff agrees, on the next Sunday display the rock in the front entryway of the church. It will be a great conversation-starter for your students, their families, and the entire church. Afterward, keep it in a corner of your youth room permanently.

End the night with prayer.

FULL OF HOT AIR
(TAMING THE TONGUE)

WHAT IT'S ALL ABOUT

Gulp! . . . "I shouldn't have said that!" Ever had that feeling as soon as something came tumbling out of your mouth?

Everyone has had one of those moments where they say something extremely stupid—and suddenly it's too late and the damage is done. This youth night deals with those moments and how to zip our lips before we've lit a fire—the kind James talks about—that we can't put out. More important, your students will consider the importance of harnessing their speech and using it to build people up, not tear them down.

Get It Started

What's needed: *several cans of alphabet soup*, a *long table*, *four cake pans*, and we suggest a *tablecloth*

This one may make you hungry, and it's guaranteed to be messy, but your kids will love it. Set up the cake pans for four teams of two to four students each. The tablecloth is to catch the many spills and dribbles sure to come.

Tell your students they have three minutes to come up with as many words as they can by using the letters from the soup. They'll find that it's more difficult than they think to come up with words. Give a can of soup to each member of the winning team!

When you're done, you may want to challenge someone to sing a song using all the words from the winning team; this can be pretty funny.

For a couple of minutes afterward, talk about how hard it can be to come up with the right words in our daily conversations. Explain that this is at least part of what this lesson is about.

Where It's Found in the Bible

James 3:3, 5-8

When we put bits into the mouths of horses to make them obey us, we can turn the whole animal. . . . Likewise the tongue is a small part of the body, but it makes great boasts. Consider what a great forest is set on fire by a small spark. The tongue also is a fire, a world of evil among the parts of the body. It corrupts the whole person, sets the whole course of his life on fire, and is itself set on fire by hell.

All kinds of animals, birds, reptiles and creatures of the sea are being tamed and have been tamed by man, but no man can tame the tongue. It is a restless evil, full of deadly poison.

YOUTH TALK OUTLINE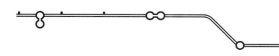

1. It's So Small

a. Just one wrong move

Why did I say that!? Has that ever gone through your head? You ask a woman when her baby is due . . . *Gulp!* She's not pregnant! You give a quick answer in school and everyone looks at you cross-eyed and you realize you weren't listening to the question. You share a secret with a blabbermouth and as soon as you finish you realize the whole world will now know. Or worse, you're asked how that new outfit looks on your friend and you share your honest opinion—only to watch her get crushed. Why *did* you say that? There's something to be said for honesty—but there's also something to be said for sensitivity.

Careless words are spoken every day and with those words we can create heartache and hurt. Someone once said that spoken words are like tearing open a feather pillow on a windy day while standing on a mountaintop—no matter what you do, you can never get those words back. No matter how bad you feel, no matter how hard you try, they are gone—free to roam and wreak havoc.

Have you ever been the victim of a careless word? A few little words and your whole day goes screaming into reverse. Those words are all you can think about. You may get called fat or skinny or dumb or ugly—or, worse—fat *and* dumb or skinny *and* ugly. You spend your day staring in the mirror wondering why people say the things they say, but it doesn't help.

In truth, we are all guilty of careless words. The Bible is clear that following Jesus means controlling our words as well as other areas of our lives. Ephesians 4:29 says that our speech should not tear people down but only be "helpful for building others up according to their needs."

FOR DISCUSSION WITH YOUR GROUP:

- Can you remember a time when what you said was hurtful to someone else, even if you didn't mean it that way?
- Can you remember a time the words you said to someone else encouraged them and gave them inspiration? How did that feel for both of you?
- What about a time in which *you* received encouraging words? How did it make a difference in your day?

b. I need a do-over!

Years ago there was a TV commercial in which a beer truck driver is on the road and a carful of girls pulls up alongside him and he gets distracted by all these good-looking women and drives off the road, crashing his truck. It looks terrible, but then the commercial pulls back and you realize he's been in a driving simulator and just failed his truck driver's test.

Don't you wish we could have the same luxury in life when it comes to our words? A do-over? Or, if you find yourself making a mistake your fist would suddenly pop into your mouth and you'd get a second or even third chance. But life, unfortunately, does not often give us this option. It'd be great if it did, but it doesn't.

It is so important to know how careless words can cause untold pain and hurt in people's lives. This is why James the brother of Jesus said that a few words can be like a small spark that sets a huge forest on fire. We may say that careless words are just little things that don't really matter, but they *do* matter to God.

But words that encourage people make all the difference. Proverbs 6:24 says, "Pleasant words are a honeycomb, sweet to the soul and healing to the bones."

BURST:

BRANDED:

2. A Little Goes a Long Way

a. Taming the tiger in all of us

It's interesting that God, through James, speaks of the animal world and how even the beasts of the earth can be tamed. The horse can be steered with a simple bit in its mouth, but without it he is in charge. Maybe we all have some kind of similar animal instinct inside us? Maybe we need a spiritual bit in our mouths to stay out of trouble with our tongues. All kinds of animals and birds and reptiles and even the largest or most dangerous of animals can be controlled—ever see a snake handler control a huge python?—but we have trouble controlling our tongues.

Think of all the trouble we could have spared ourselves of if we had kept ourselves from saying dumb things. Have you ever found yourself in a mess of trouble, wishing you hadn't said something? We can all relate.

BURST:

BRANDED:

b. Bite your lip

God says something interesting in James 3, verse 8: "No man can tame the tongue." So what are we supposed to do? Should we duct tape our mouths shut? Stick a candy bar in our mouths before we speak so we have time to think it over? It's a fun thought but it's not practical and we would gain way too much weight. So if man can't tame the tongue, who can? Good question.

We see in James 3, verse 17 that good words come from above. James wrote that "the wisdom that comes from heaven is first of all pure, then peace-loving, considerate" and a number of other good things that encourage other people. So how do we get words from above down into our mouths? First they have to come into our hearts. But before they get to our hearts they have to come from our minds. It's pretty simple when we think about it. What we spend our time thinking about is what gets planted in our hearts and what grows in our hearts comes out of our mouths. So we must pay careful attention to put the right things into our minds and hearts.

All of us are farmers in a strange way; we all reap a harvest every day. The harvest is seen coming out of our mouths through our words. So what are you harvesting? What is the fruit of your mouth? The only way to change the harvest is to change what is planted. A farmer would be considered crazy if he planted corn and then got mad when corn is what came up from the earth! He could yell and scream and stomp his feet and demand that the dirt grow wheat, but if it's not what he planted, wheat is not going to happen. In the same way, if we get mad at ourselves over the careless words that slip past our lips, then we first have to take a close look at what we're planting.

FOR DISCUSSION:

- Why does God say that true wisdom comes only "from heaven"?
- What should we be planting in our minds and hearts each day?

3. The Language of Heaven

a. A tuneup before you talk

Have you ever listened to a car that's in desperate need of a tuneup? It sounds horrible! That thing will stutter, sputter, and waste gas as if there was a hole in the gas tank. It needs a tuneup! Ever watch what a good mechanic does? He starts up the engine and listens closely before he does anything else. Often, just by his ear alone, he can pinpoint the problem. Then he goes to work.

Imagine yourself as that mechanic—but think tuneup to your heart and thoughts, not to a car. Take some time to listen to your words from the past few weeks. What do they sound like? Did you stutter, sputter, and waste a lot of words on useless and careless talk? If you really want an honest opinion, ask some of the people in your life—parents, a mentor, your friends, your teacher—to weigh in with a diagnosis of your words.

Then go to God and ask for a tuneup of the heart. He can give us a daily and weekly schedule of needed upkeep, just like what's needed for a car. God may say you need to add more of his Word going into your mind on a daily basis. He may suggest you no longer hang with certain friends who are filling your mind with not-so-healthy things. He may show you that you need to go and ask for forgiveness of something careless that you've spoken in the past. But all of it will be worth it.

BURST:

BRANDED:

b. How to make our words really count

Ever try to speak with someone who doesn't speak your language and you don't speak theirs? It can be very frustrating and not very productive.

God may sometimes think we're a little like that. His heart is: It's not that hard; I just want you to speak my language. There are lives out there to touch and hurting people that you can help, but you don't speak my language. Listen, and I will teach you the right way to speak!

Our words are extremely important. They get God's message of faith, hope, and love out to a lost and hurting world. But this only happens if we take the time to learn his Word, to pray, and to seek his heart for the lost. When we do these things, we're learning to speak his language. How many times would you have changed how you talked if you knew God was sitting next to you? Guess what? He is!

FOR DISCUSSION:

- Where do you need a tuneup in your daily walk with God?
- How would that tuneup affect how you speak?

Wrap It Up

Today is a great day to take the time to pray and tell God about the careless words you have used. Spend some time thinking about how your words have caused careless sparks—but instead can be turned into words that bring healing and hope to hurting people.

ALTERED

What's needed: A *helium balloon* for as many students as will be in attendance; *markers* (we recommend them with wider and/or softer tips, not sharp tips, as those could start bursting all those balloons!)

Have a helium balloon at the altar area for each student. Invite them to come forward, pick up a balloon and marker, and write down, first, some of the careless words they've said to others, and second, careless words that have been said to them. Ask your students to take time to pray and ask God about these careless words that were once free to wander and cause pain—produced both by them and by others.

Then take everyone outside and release the balloons—and the wandering words written on them—to heaven.

End the night in prayer.

NEW YIELD RESOLUTIONS
(GAINING BY GIVING UP)

WHAT IT'S ALL ABOUT

Most people like the New Year's Eve holiday. The parties, the food, the countdown—they're all energizing. Lots of people also love writing out their New Year's resolutions—but not many are good at keeping them. How many times have you heard someone say they wish they could start over in the middle of the year and do things over?

Your students will understand that, with God, we always have the opportunity to do just that.

Instead of New Year's resolutions you'll be challenging them to make New Yield resolutions. *What?*, you say. The idea is that rather than going after things they want for the new year they'll be challenged to yield things to God in their continued discipleship to his Son.

Get It Started

What's needed: Either use *fake money* from one of the many board games that use it or print up your own fake money (see below for the amount you'll need); a good idea is to have *magazine pictures* or *little toys, trinkets, or actual items themselves* (such as shoes or CDs) of the things your students will be "shopping" for

(Fun idea: If you print up your own funny money, put the faces of your student ministry volunteers on one side of the "bills.")

This meeting is all about giving up—though it won't seem like it at first. Pass out the fake money to your students as they come in to youth group. Give them all the same amount—$1,000—and tell them they're about to go on a shopping spree. You then go through a list of items and find out what they're willing to spend their money on. Make up your own "shopping list," but it can include things like:

- Acne eraser: $100
- A best friend: that'll cost you $300!
- New shoes: $75
- A brother or sister: $50 (a bargain, or not?)
- Used car: $500, please
- iPod: $150
- CD of your choice: $20
- Big screen TV: $750 and it's yours!
- An entirely new wardrobe: $800
- New parents: $1,000
- A new pet: $200 (and explain that they'll also be paying $50 a month for the rest of the pet's life)
- A cool new cell phone with a full keyboard: $250, including cost of the first two months of the contract
- Pack of string cheese: $5 (unlimited quantities!)
- And as many more as you want to add . . .

Your students get a chance to buy anything on the list within their budget; they must hand in their money to do so. (Make sure you have "change" if it's needed.) It's always interesting—and a little revealing—to see who's a taker of which items (such as who would want a new brother or sister). When they're all out of money, or close to it, have students stand up and "show off" their new items and tell why they bought what they bought.

But the kicker is that this meeting is about giving up—not getting.

Where It's Found in the Bible

Romans 12:1, 2

Therefore, I urge you, brothers, in view of God's mercy, to offer your bodies as living sacrifices, holy and pleasing to God—this is your spiritual act of worship. Do not conform any longer to the pattern of this world, but be transformed by the renewing of your mind. Then you will be able to test and approve what God's will is—his good, pleasing and perfect will.

YOUTH TALK OUTLINE

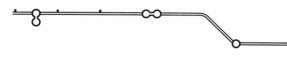

1. What's in a Sign?

    a. Someone else can follow those signs!

       A simple and well-known fact: Driving safely requires doing what the road signs say. This means we have to yield to and even obey their commands. What happens if, one day, you just decide you're not going to follow road signs any longer? You're sick and tired of people telling you what to do, so you just snap and drive any way you want. Well, after they release you from the hospital, or after you get that ticket, or worst of all, after they pull your body from the car, you might have a different mind-set about that choice. Safety in a car comes from yielding to all the signs on the road—and not just the "Yield" signs.

As followers of Christ our lives draw similar parallels. We chose to become Christians but in no time flat our choices can become about what we want to do and when we want to do it, or what things we think we deserve in life. We hear the preachers on TV who make it sound like Christianity is a big piñata and if you hit it enough with a Jesus stick you get all you want and then some.

But this is not the spirit of Christ's gospel. Jesus said we must be willing to pick up our cross and yield our lives to him to get what we truly need and want. It's not about what we can get out of life. The opening activity was about taking a glimpse into where our priorities can lie. But the bottom line for a follower of Christ is that we have to be willing, first and foremost, to give.

BURST:

BRANDED:

b. Gotta plant, gotta yield

"The good man brings good things out of the good stored up in his heart, and the evil man brings evil things out of the evil stored up in his heart. For out of the overflow of his heart his mouth speaks" (Luke 6:45).

When a farmer expects a crop to grow, he does a very simple thing: he yields to, or puts his trust in, God's design for growth. He puts the seeds in the ground and, without seeing them or being guaranteed of anything, he waters all that soil, fertilizes it, and then waits. . . . When his crops begin to grow he understands he must not open them too soon. He has to wait until they are fully mature or he won't yield a harvest.

If he digs up the seed, or tears open those new young ears of corn, or begins to pick those beans before they're ready, he's not going to yield anything close to a true harvest. So what he does is yield to God and God's plan for nature and simply awaits the outcome.

Sometimes we lack that kind of patience—we start to yield, but then we take over in the middle of the process. We never quite figure out why we don't get the full harvest of good things we'd like in our lives.

FOR DISCUSSION WITH YOUR GROUP:

Let's talk through a few examples together:

- We promise ourselves we're going to trust God, to yield, in that class at school or at youth group or on the sports team or in the club. We'll hold our tongues this time and not say a word . . . and then we slip and let words spill all over the place. We damage our reputation or standing in the group.
  Have you ever had something like this happen? Can you share?

- We think, *This time I'm going to trust God that my Dad or Mom will soften up if I show them respect . . .* but then we slip, we don't yield to God, we badger our parents, or nag, or say something in disrespect.
  Have you ever had something like this happen? Can you share?
- Or we promise we're going to trust God—to yield—in finding a boyfriend or girlfriend . . . and pretty soon we're manipulating our relationships and slipping into bad habits all over again.
  Have you ever had something like this happen? Can you share?

2. Hey, That's Mine!

a. Everybody else has one

"Everybody else has one!" Have you ever had those words come out of your mouth? We live in a world of entitlements, a world in which people expect to get, get, get.

To be deprived is unthinkable, especially self-imposed deprivation! <u>We too often think: Why would anyone, ever, give up their rights? It just does not make sense in today's world.</u>

<u>In contrast, God calls us not to be of this world but only to live in it.</u>

Isabel Maxey lived that way. It was 1937, and Isabel was a young woman determined to go to China for mission work. There were many obstacles. And it didn't help when she learned that she would be living so far into the country's interior—traveling on pack mules to get there—and in such primitive conditions. She knew there could be scary consequences if she were to come down with serious dental infections; she was completely removed from any proper medical care. Snow and distance would make treatments all but impossible. But Isabel didn't give up her plans. Instead, she had all her teeth pulled before leaving for China! She was willing to sacrifice her own smile to take Jesus to the people of China. Isabel understood the principal of giving up her privileges for the sake of others.[2]

What is God saying to you? Maybe he's calling you to yield a boyfriend or girlfriend relationship that isn't doing either of you any good. Maybe it's a habit or a job or even an attitude. Maybe he's calling you to consider yielding to a life of missions or service?

Most likely he is calling you to simply yield to his voice and to his leading every day!

BURST:

BRANDED:

b. Whose hands are you offered to?

Let's go back to our main Scripture for tonight. This would be a good one to memorize in view of the culture in which we live:

Do not conform any longer to the pattern of this world, but be transformed by the renewing of your mind. Then you will be able to test and approve what God's will is—his good, pleasing and perfect will [Romans 12:2].

Have you ever heard someone say "read, pray, and obey"? It's a phrase that's often been used, and seems cliché, but this is the mind-set of the person who yields to Christ. In Romans 6, the apostle Paul had more to say:

Do not offer the parts of your body to sin, as instruments of wickedness, but rather offer yourselves to God, as those who have been brought from death to life (Romans 6:13).

And,

Don't you know that when you offer yourselves to someone to obey him as slaves, you are slaves to the one whom you obey—whether you are slaves to sin, which leads to death, or to obedience, which leads to righteousness (Romans 6:16).

What all this really means is to yield yourself to God. Ever been in the car with your little brother or sister and they start copying you? It can drive you nuts, but guess what? It's biblical. God says that we should yield to him or, rather, *copy* him. So we have to read, pray, and obey so that we can yield to God—or copy him—in this life.

Or are we yielding to—or copying—someone or something else?

We decide to yield to someone or something every day. Whose hands are we putting our lives in? Think of it this way:

- A basketball in most people's hands is worth about $19—but put it in the hands of Lebron James and it's worth $33 million
- A baseball in most hands is worth $6—in the hands of Alex Rodriguez it's worth $200 million or more
- A big stick, or staff, in your hands will help you hike a trail—but a staff in Moses' hands will part a mighty sea
- Two fish and five loaves of bread in the hands of anyone on earth is a couple of fish sandwiches—two fish and five loaves of bread in the hands of Jesus is a meal for thousands
- Nails in your hands might work well to build a birdhouse—in Jesus' hands they produce salvation for anyone in the world who will accept his gift

FOR DISCUSSION:

- What skills, abilities, or resources of yours are you putting in God's hands?
- How can you more fully offer your life to him?

Wrap It Up

God is asking us to yield all areas of our lives to him. At the front, near the altar area, you'll find yellow "Yield" signs, enough for each person to take at least one, pray to God over, and

on the back write out the areas in which you believe God is calling you to yield. Listen quietly to his voice and be willing to give up in order to get what he has in mind for you.

ALTERED

What's needed: Have plenty of *"Yield" signs* printed up for your students to write on (make sure they're on yellow paper and mimic the look of the "Yield" signs you see in traffic); have a *number of extras*, as well, in case students want to start over or fill up another sheet; *pens or markers*

Challenge your students to list out the areas in which they need to yield to God. Then ask them to carry these signs in their Bibles, cars, in a notebook, or place them on a mirror at home.

End the night with prayer.

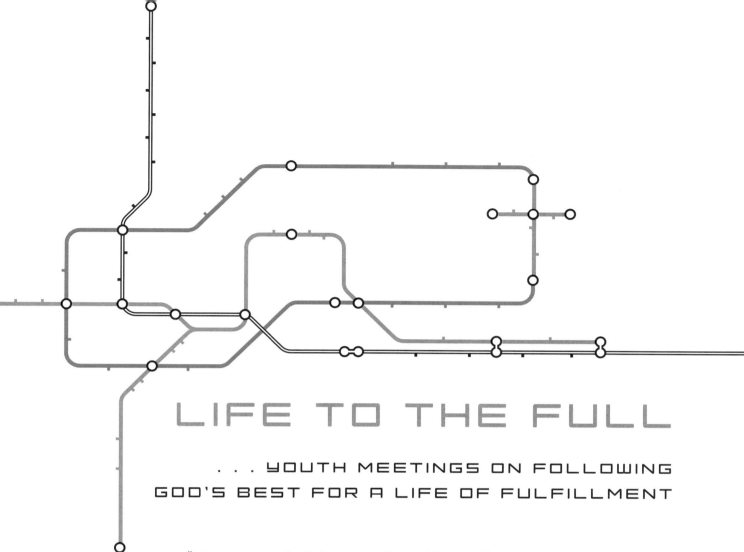

LIFE TO THE FULL

. . . YOUTH MEETINGS ON FOLLOWING GOD'S BEST FOR A LIFE OF FULFILLMENT

"I have come that they may have life, and have it to the full. I am the good shepherd. The good shepherd lays down his life for the sheep."

—John 10:10, 11

. . . Instead, be filled with the Spirit.

—Ephesians 5:18

SURPRISE PARTY (IS THERE ANY GREATER GIFT THAN GRACE?)

WHAT IT'S ALL ABOUT

Everybody loves a good party—especially when it's a surprise party thrown for them! Friends, gifts, pictures, food, cake, and more make it a memorable event. This youth talk will serve up a surprise party for someone who totally isn't expecting it. Trust us, watching their reaction will be priceless!

But what's way more surprising than any party any person can throw is God's gift of grace toward us. It's undeserved, there is no way it can be earned, and it's quite a shock when we understand what he's done for us as sinners.

In this meeting, you're going to surprise someone and, in turn, surprise your whole group with a deeper insight into God's undeserved love and grace.

Get It Started

What's needed: Behind some back or side doors or, in the next room, you'll need a party just waiting to bust out: *a cake, some party music, a few gifts, balloons, and streamers*; another leader or member of your youth group will be waiting to *interrupt your talk with a note*; with some forethought, *choose one student* (who you know will be in attendance!)—this might be someone needing encouragement but also a person who doesn't embarrass easily

Option: have some *people ready with cameras* to take pictures of this mini-party

Tell your students this meeting is going to kick off with your talk. Get started, but then, just a few minutes in, have someone interrupt things and hand you a note. Now, play this for some drama. Tell your students this is important and that you're going to . . . invite one student up front for a surprise party! Call that student up front.

Give them no particular reason; just tell them they've been selected for a party.

Then have your leaders bring in the cake, the gifts, the food, play party music and, if you want, have people taking pictures. Pandemonium is what you're shooting for here!

After a couple of minutes of shock for this student, slow everything down and wrap up the party. In front of everyone, ask the student why this party was thrown for them—they probably will have no idea.

Even if they think they know, tell them all the reasons they're guessing are incorrect.

Have everyone sit down and tell your students the reason will be obvious in a few minutes.

Where It's Found in the Bible

Ephesians 1:7

In him we have redemption through his blood, the forgiveness of sins, in accordance with the riches of God's grace.

YOUTH TALK OUTLINE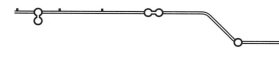

1. Everyone Loves a Good Party

a. Surprise!

What's the greatest surprise you've ever received? Was it a party, a gift, a visitor, or maybe someone jumping out of your locker? The best surprises are the ones that catch us totally off guard and are undeserved. Let's face it: If you know a surprise is coming, then it's not really a surprise at all. Or if you think you deserve it, that takes some of the fun out of it as well. A true surprise is, well, a surprise!

God is a God of surprises. Maybe you don't think of him that way, but this is true and it's a part of his character. He gives us a free gift, called salvation, and it's something we don't deserve, can't earn, and definitely don't completely comprehend. He even paid for this gift with the life of his own son.

What's the most you've ever gone through to surprise someone? What's the most it's ever cost you? Think of planning a fantastic party for a friend; you go through weeks of preparation. You work extra hours at your job and you just know your friend will be totally blown away. The day arrives and so do all the people. The cars are all parked blocks away. Everyone hides and the lights are off. You and your friends are ready to jump out and yell "Surprise!!!" when the door begins to open. The moment's finally here. Your friend steps in, is completely caught off guard, and your party is under way!

Now it's in full roar and your friend stops you in the middle of everything and asks, "So what's this for?" You tell him it's because you and your friends love him and you just wanted to make him feel special, to encourage him. He asks, why him? What did he do? But you just keep telling him it's because you all love him. He sees all the gifts and all the people and is still confused; he tells you he doesn't deserve this. You tell him you know that, but you wanted to throw this party so he'd know how many people care for him.

Imagine your friend in that situation. He'd be pretty blown away.

FOR DISCUSSION WITH YOUR GROUP:

- Have you guys ever thrown, or had thrown for you, a surprise party?
- What were your feelings? What were your friends' feelings?

b. Uh, can you pay me back for all this trouble?

Want the secret of how to ruin a great surprise party? After it's over give the bill to the person you threw the party for! Tell them you planned it and spent lots of money and time on this thing but now you expect him to take care of all that cost. You also expect him to clean your room, wash your dog, and baby-sit your sister. Safe to say this would not be a good ending to that party.

We wouldn't do that, right? But let's go way bigger: God threw us a party that cost his Son everything—way more than time and money—and he doesn't expect us to pay him back. In fact, there's no way we could. It's way too expensive. No matter how hard we tried, there'd be no way to repay the debt. And there would have been no way, no how, that we could have seen getting ourselves out of our state of sin. That's why it's such a great surprise—we never saw it coming. We, the undeserving, get the best gift of all—and that's eternal life and a relationship with him.

BURST:

BRANDED:

2. You Can't Afford It

a. How much would you save?

Start this section with discussion questions:
- How much are you willing to save up to buy something you really want? Maybe a hundred, or five hundred, or even a thousand dollars?
- What's the most expensive thing you've ever saved your money for?
- How much would you save to buy a gift for someone else?
- How much would you be willing to save in order to buy your own life, if it were in danger? (Note to youth leader: Yes, that's a bit of a trick question!)

Yeah, all of us would save as much as we had to in order to buy our own life, or to gain our freedom, if we had to. But the truth is that we are held for ransom—by our sin, which causes separation from a holy God. And the truth also is that we don't have what it takes to pay the ransom price. Christ, however, could pay that price by offering his sinless life. The great news—the surprise—is that he did, in fact, pay the full price for us.

People cannot be good enough, strong enough, or nice enough to earn God's forgiveness. It's a free gift. Entirely.

b. All are invited

All of us have seen one of those TV game shows where someone walks away with thousands of dollars in prizes. They may have been audience members who didn't really expect to get on stage. A pretty sweet surprise! But a far greater surprise is the surprise party that God has for us.

To come to God's party you don't need a special invitation, or to have won your way there through an audition; really, you don't need any reason at all! You just simply need to accept his invitation to attend this incredible event. And there are gifts! Everyone receives a relationship with the maker of the universe, eternal life, grace, peace, mercy, goodness, love—the list goes on and on. And the best part is that absolutely anyone can accept this invitation.

BURST:

BRANDED:

3. He Can Afford It

a. He paid the debt—for his enemies

No one could afford the party that God put on except his own Son, Jesus. He knew it would cost him his life and he still planned it, the Bible says, from the beginning of time. Revelation 13:8 calls Jesus "the Lamb that was slain from the creation of the world"—this basically means that his death was planned even before man was created. God in his wisdom could see the fall of man and had already planned a response! That's deep stuff, but what the Bible teaches!

The price he paid was a sinless life that led him to a painful, horrible death on the cross. Even if we wanted to we couldn't pay this price because none of us are sinless. And the truth is that none of us would be willing to die for those around us who we feel didn't deserve it. How many of us want to give up our lives for a murderer, a drug addict, or even the mean girl at school? Never! This is what the apostle Paul wrote in Romans 5:10 when he said that Jesus died for us "when we were God's enemies." This is part of the surprise that God had in store for us. He died for everyone, and that includes all of us, who chose sin, who chose to live separated from a holy God.

FOR DISCUSSION:

- How do we normally act toward those we consider enemies?
- Why is it difficult to think of *loving* someone you'd consider an enemy?
- What little steps could you take this week to begin to show love toward someone who has felt like an enemy to you?

b. An unopened gift is no gift at all

What if you walked into your friend's house and saw a Christmas tree surrounded by hundreds of gifts? She quickly explains that every year her family buys tons of gifts—but no one ever opens them. You might first shake her and then tell her that her family has to open the gifts! She seems unconvinced. After trying some more, you finally give up, thinking she's lost her mind. Ridiculous, right? But the same thing happens in the lives of many people every day—God's given them a gift, but they refuse to open it.

This is one gift you have to make sure you open. This is one gift you have to make sure your friends know about!

BURST:

BRANDED:

Wrap It Up

As we wrap up, everyone gets a chance to celebrate their own party! This party has been set and the invitation has been given: You may have already accepted Christ and, if you have, this is all the more reason to take advantage of the opportunity and celebrate God's goodness.

Maybe you haven't accepted God's invitation; that makes his call to you even more important.

This meeting is about throwing a party, for two reasons—either to celebrate all that God's done for you, or to celebrate God's invitation to you to come into a relationship with him. You may need to learn more, you may have more study of the Bible to do, but you can still celebrate God's great love and his great invitation!

ALTERED

What's needed: More of the same from the start of the evening: *food, cake, music, streamers, balloons, possibly gifts*—whatever works!

The end of this meeting should be one big party. Invite students to eat food and cake, hang out, and celebrate God's grace. Take plenty of pictures that you can show over the next few weeks.

End the night with prayer.

FEAR, FEATHERS, AND FAITH (NOTHING TO BE AFRAID OF)

WHAT IT'S ALL ABOUT

Mice, snakes, poison ivy, heights, roller coasters, public speaking, the opposite sex—everyone is afraid of something! Fear can be a good thing, but it can also be crippling. And if we don't get a handle on it we'll never truly enjoy life. To live in fear is not God's best for us and it's not what he wants for us!

In the Psalms, both Moses and David give us direction in how to face our fears—through turning to God's covering. Fear not, God's feathers—and increased faith in your group—are on the way.

Note: This lesson has discussion questions more heavily weighted toward the front of the meeting. This is a great topic to get students talking—but being open about your life, first, will greatly help.

Get It Started

What's needed: *Blank paper* and *pens or markers*; if you're feeling ambitious, videotape some *random interviews on this topic* with people around town (see below)

What are you afraid of? This is a two-part icebreaker that can start as soon as your students walk into the room. As they enter, have them take a blank piece of paper and list three things they're afraid of.

Listing your own fears on a board up front, or on an overhead, will greatly help get things rolling. Be vulnerable so your students will! Lists may include things like the fear of public speaking, the fear of heights, the fear of spiders—students may fear any number of things.

Then, with students' permission, read a handful of these before your talk. You'll want to keep these anonymous!

Option: Another way to have fun is to see if others in the group can guess who wrote down which list of fears. You'll need to tell your students beforehand that you want to do it this way, however. Keep in mind that a number of students may be more guarded in their lists if you go this route.

Option: Do you have a friend who can shoot video? Want to see if you can do a man-on-the-street like Leno? Then this is pretty cool: Spend some time walking around your town asking people what they fear. Play the video as part of the activity. You're sure to hear some silly stuff!

Where It's Found in the Bible

Psalm 91:3-11
Surely he will save you from the fowler's snare
and from the deadly pestilence.

He will cover you with his feathers,
and under his wings you will find refuge;
his faithfulness will be your shield and rampart.

You will not fear the terror of night,
nor the arrow that flies by day

nor the pestilence that stalks in the darkness,
nor the plague that destroys at midday.

A thousand may fall at your side,
ten thousand at your right hand,
but it will not come near you.

You will only observe with your eyes
and see the punishment of the wicked.

If you make the Most High your dwelling—
even the Lord, who is my refuge—

then no harm will befall you,
no disaster will come near your tent.

For he will command his angels concerning you
to guard you in all your ways.

YOUTH TALK OUTLINE

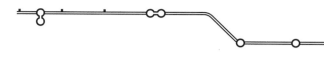

1. Fear This

a. What are you afraid of?

Have you ever heard of people who are deathly afraid of feet? They exist—people afraid of feet! You thought your fears were bad! There are some weird fears out there. Take Tachophobia for example. No, this is not the fear of Mexican food with a hard shell! It's the fear of speed. But with this fear we're not only talking about, for instance, going 100 miles per hour in a car; people who have this fear are even afraid of walking too fast! Then there is pupaphobia. Not making this up: it's the fear of puppets. We may think these fears are ridiculous and wonder what a puppet could possibly do to ever hurt someone.

FOR DISCUSSION WITH YOUR GROUP:

- Why do you think people have fears and phobias?
- What was the last thing you feared that actually came true?
- Do the things you fear tend to be realistic or irrational?
- Do you think God cares about our fears, even if they're silly to other people?

Most of the time what we fear never happens. Take the person who fears puppets; we can probably say with certainty that no one has ever been carjacked by a puppet, held up at the ATM machine by a marionette, or beaten up by a sock puppet! Yet, at the same time, you can find online sites that say millions of people around the world have serious fears of . . . puppets.

We all have our fears and too often we hang on to them as if what we're afraid of is going to happen to us at any time. Even if it's a rational fear like heights, you rarely find yourself standing on top of a huge mountain, building, or riding in a hot air balloon. In fact, unless you get balloon-jacked, you won't end up in a hot air balloon unless you decide to go up in one!

BURST:

BRANDED:

b. What is FEAR? What is faith?

When you were younger, ever see something absolutely crazy in the dark when you couldn't fall asleep in your room? Say, a psycho clown on a unicorn with a sword and a bag of jelly beans ready to attack you. Then when you finally mustered up enough courage to wriggle out of bed and over to the light switch to turn on the light, you found out that odd shape was a towel lying on your desk with the lamp behind it. Nothing changed except the light was turned on!

Someone once said the definition for *FEAR* could be this: "false evidence appearing real." That's a great definition because that's what fears often are—things that aren't real that appear to be real. <u>What we fear is what we focus on and that focus affects our behavior.</u>

In truth, fear is faith working backwards. We believe in something, thinking it will come true, and it's usually based on false, useless information. Living by faith is living just the opposite!

- Do you think the definitions of fear, as just given, are good ones? Agree or disagree and why?
- We tend to think of faith as "believing in something we can't see." But faith often seems to encompass things bigger than that. As you see it, what's the best definition of faith?
- Why is it so much easier to fear than to have faith?

2. Everyone's Afraid

a. But there's a place to turn

OK, let's go way back. Maybe you had experiences like this: It's first grade, and a kid picks on you and you run home to Dad or Mom and cry for help. It's human instinct at that age to run to a parent when times get tough. But really, we have the same instinct when we face fear in our lives today. We want help, relief, rescue. We want pulled out of that fear and pulled out *now*.

For many of us, as smaller kids, we used to think that Dad or Mom could solve any problem. But there are some problems or issues that even our parents can't help with. There are certain things in life where we know we have to go deeper—to God and God alone—but even then we can wait and wait and wait and turn to other things before going to him.

Psalm 91, verse 9 tells us that if we make God our dwelling place we can find a place of refuge in him. Refuge: "a place of shelter or protection from danger or distress." Who doesn't need a refuge at times in life? But is it possible that we don't turn to God first because we haven't made him our dwelling place—the place where we live—to begin with?

We get busy and choose to live in our music, in front of the computer, in our activities, with our friends, or in front of the TV—but not really in God's presence. When trouble hits we feel awkward about going to God; it's only when our backs are to the wall that we approach his throne.

This isn't God's best for us! He doesn't want us to fear or feel overwhelmed, as Psalm 91 shows us. Jesus said in John 10:10 that he came so we would have the greatest life—"life to the full."

- It's worth thinking over your life to make sure you're ready and in God's presence when trouble and fear strike. Where do you usually turn?

- What does a refuge mean to you? Friends can make a great refuge, but how can God be a refuge we can turn to at any time?

b. The place for protection

"I promise the lowest-price-guarantee, guaranteed!" Those are the kinds of promises made at used car dealerships, aren't they? Not exactly businesses known for honesty and integrity. If we read this psalm, Psalm 91, and at the bottom it was signed by "Harold, used car salesman," it would be hard to put a great deal of faith in it, wouldn't it? But this psalm is way different because it's a promise coming from God through man. We're not sure if this psalm was written by Moses or David (many scholars think David), but <u>one thing rings true: the writer is speaking from experience. He has felt God's protection in times of fear.</u>

"Feather power to the rescue!" is what this is all about. Verse 4 gives us a beautiful, and prophetic, picture of Jesus and his protection over us. God really wants the best for us! Look at verse 4 again:

He will cover you with his feathers,
and under his wings you will find refuge;
his faithfulness will be your shield and rampart.

This verse says that God—somewhat like the picture of a mother bird, or a mother hen, protecting her young—will put his wings out over us and protect us. In the same way, Christ spread out his hands on a cross and died for us so that we can be assured of his protection. He died because he loves us, and "perfect love drives out fear," as 1 John 4:18 says. That's God's best for us!

BURST:

BRANDED:

3. Overcoming

a. Facing down the final fear

So we say, "Great. He will cover me in times of trouble and fear." But can we then fear—yes, *fear*—that with an assurance like that we'll blow it and let God down? Of course we can!

But if we don't have to fear then we don't need to question how God will choose to use us. We can pray, share our faith with people, speak up for Christ, believe he will work in our lives—and *know* that we're covered.

BURST:

BRANDED:

b. You've got the ironman suit

Picture it like this: If you had an ironman suit that would protect you in any situation and you chose not to help others, or to protect only yourself, you would be seen as evil, as the villain in any story.

But you've got such a suit, a spiritual suit, and God *will* use you! You don't have to worry about how. Just step out on faith and let God use you exactly as he wants. Is it easy? No. But it begins with trusting your life in the hands of the one who gave you that life.

Wrap It Up

Have you ever been asked this question: If you could do anything and not fail, what would you choose to do? That's a great question! God may work out your success differently than the way you saw it happening, but if you and I believe we don't have to fear, what would we plan to do for Christ?

What is it that you know you need to do for him but just have not yet pulled the trigger on?

ALTERED

What's needed: A *pile of feathers* picked up from a local craft store—or you can pluck some chickens (we suggest the trip to the craft store); perhaps some appropriate *mood music*

Ask your students to come forward and spend some time in prayer, giving God all their fears. Play some appropriate music.

Tell your students that, in exchange for giving their fears to God, they will grab a feather and place it in their Bibles or journal. It can be a bookmark to remind them that God is there to cover every fear and to protect them in times of trouble.

End the night with prayer.

COVERED IN GOD'S KINGDOM (WE'VE GOT YOUR BACK)

WHAT IT'S ALL ABOUT

It's a great feeling to know that someone has your back. You can call that friend at any time and know they'll be there for you.

But there is no better feeling than to know that the body of Christ has your back, that your friends in God's kingdom have got you covered. This youth meeting will help explain how we can build friendships that last—the type that transcend normal relationships and instead become kingdom-transforming ones. And the type that help build God's church at the same time.

Get It Started

What's needed: Virtually nothing: only *a little pre-thought* on those in your group who might consider themselves best friends, and why

Option: *Write out your questions on index cards* before the meeting

This one's always fun: You're going to give your students a best friend quiz! Invite up front two people at a time who call themselves best friends. Sit them back-to-back (it's amazing what good friends can communicate nonverbally!) and, with absolutely no talking allowed, have one friend write his or her answers to the questions. After the answer is written, ask the other friend to verbally answer what she believes are her friend's preferences.

What you'll find out is how much they *really* know about each other. (Note: Bring up front only a couple of pairs so that no one feels left out.)

Ask basic questions like: favorite color? Favorite music? Favorite band? Food? Movie? Dog or cat person? . . . and then turn to the increasingly hard or ridiculous! Does she know what her best friend eats for breakfast? Fried rice or steamed? Does she journal or not?

Her favorite book of the Bible? Is he a WWE (World Wrestling Entertainment) or MMA (mixed martial arts) guy? Does he like burgers or dogs?

After you're done, point out to your students that even best friends don't know everything about each other. What they *do* have that joins them is simply that they've chosen to be good friends; the bond of friendship runs much deeper than trivial preferences.

Where It's Found in the Bible

2 Samuel 1:11, 12

Then David and all the men with him took hold of their clothes and tore them. They mourned and wept and fasted till evening for Saul and his son Jonathan . . . because they had fallen by the sword.

YOUTH TALK OUTLINE

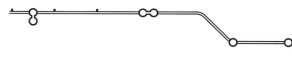

1. Yeah, You Can Choose Your Friends

   a. Pick someone

      So you have a choice to make about who you want to be friends with.

FOR DISCUSSION WITH YOUR GROUP:

- Who would you choose to be your friend from among this group?
  - — a rock star
  - — a multi-millionaire
  - — a professional athlete
  - — Simon, Randy, Paula, or Kara from *American Idol* (your choice)
  - — the latest winner of *American Idol*
  - — the guy down the street who works at the local supermarket bagging groceries—he looks emo and breaks your eggs way too often

- On what do you base your choice?

(**Note:** You can have some fun with this one; let your students debate the merits of being best friends with whomever they're choosing of the first five options.)

OK, so on the surface it seems like a pretty easy choice to rule out grocery-bagger boy first, right? Until, that is, you learn a lot more about this teenager who's bagging your family's bagels. Sure, he looks like a punk and he doesn't seem to have much skill other than always remembering to ask "paper or plastic?" and somehow managing to keep from squishing the bread. But then you stumble onto the deeper truth: This kid is a giant killer. His name is David and he's the youngest—and most forgotten—boy from a big family. And yes, he actually took down a giant: through his faith he took out a nine-foot-tall ugly behemoth who was making fun of God and God's army.

You get the picture: David wasn't a bagger of groceries, but he had just about the same kind of job. He watched sheep. That's all he did, all day long, before his battle with Goliath—he watched dirty, stinking sheep.

Jonathan, son of Saul, the king of Israel at the time, made the same type of choice as choosing a grocery bagger for a best friend when he first met David. The truth is, when you're the king's son you can be friends with absolutely anyone you want. And guess what: if whoever the king's son chooses knows what's good for him, he'll be his friend as well.

So in the middle of war and a crazy battle Jonathan takes notice of this teen-ager, David, who steps up to the plate and takes on the giant, Goliath, and wins. Jonathan took notice for a few reasons—which we'll get to—and quickly becomes buddies with David.

BURST:

BRANDED:

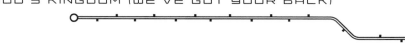

b. Why you?

What would you do if you were supposed to receive some big award but, at the last moment, it's given away to someone else, a person you don't even know? There you are, at the banquet, all dressed up in your tux and mentally preparing your speech when announcement time comes. The banquet emcee steps to the podium and, as you prepare to stand to the sounds of thunderous clapping, he says that the award goes to the person who has made the biggest impact in your city this year . . . and then he calls the name of . . . this other, younger guy, some dude you've never heard of. What would you do? How would you feel?

In ancient Israel, Jonathan did something very strange in the middle of watching David take a victory lap while gaining fame throughout the land: Jonathan celebrates with David. But he ends up going much further: not only does he celebrate with him, Jonathan encourages David's role in the grand God-scheme-of-things to come. Why did Jonathan do this? It appears Jonathan knew some things that lots of people need to learn. He wanted to be friends with David because one, he admired David's will to serve God; and two, he knew David was the best man for what God had in store for the nation of Israel.

Take a closer look for a minute—just think to yourself. Who are your closest friends? Have you chosen your friends because of their will to serve God—or out of convenience and because of what you will get from the relationship? Do you have friends who call you to what's best for your spiritual life?

Now comes the really tough question: Do your friends feel that way about you?

Jonathan not only seeks out David as a friend for the reasons we listed, he goes one better and quickly becomes David's best friend. They become incredible friends, the kind that can be separated in body but have hearts that always remain close.

2. A True Friend

a. You before me

What's the most you've ever done for someone? How about things like opening the door for someone else, washing their car, helping them with their homework, or even giving a friend some of your hard-earned money? What if you won some big contest or stood to inherit great wealth or a huge company and all the prestige that went with it, but instead of taking it you gave it to your friend because you thought they would handle it better? Impossible, you say? No one in their right mind would do this? But this is exactly what Jonathan did when he met David. Jonathan should have been next in line for the throne and all that came with it. But instead he gave it all to David because he understood that God had chosen David. That is an amazing friend!

All of us, as humans, can get it backwards when it comes to friendships. Way too often we become someone's friend for what we can get out of it. We might even argue and say that we're friends with the people we get along with . . . but still, isn't that making the choice about *us*? It's great to have friends who you love to hang with! But have you ever seen someone and thought, "I'll be their friend because I can give them encouragement, stability, hope, the things that they need"? Jesus said that a true friend is willing to lay down his or her life for another: "Greater love has no one than this, that he lay down his life for his friends" [John 15:13]. Jesus meant the physical life—but desires, hopes, and dreams can be given up, or changed, so that someone else can prosper. This was what Jonathan did. This is a true friend.

FOR DISCUSSION:

- Have you ever chosen a friend, or joined a circle of friends, for reasons that didn't feel right? Can you share about that time without using names or identifying people?
- Jonathan supported David, made efforts to save his life from his father, who was trying to kill him, and generally put David ahead of his own concerns. Why is this so hard to do? Why were these amazing choices?

b. Here . . . take my stuff!

Have you ever received clothing as a gift and faked a smile and pretended that you liked it? "Oh, what lovely, paisley, plaid, pink pants, Grandma. They are just what I wanted!" . . . You know what you're thinking: *Liar!* But what about clothes you really liked, or really needed, *badly* needed? It would sound sort of strange if you had a friend who said, "I love you so much that I'm going to give you some clothes. No, not new ones. The ones I have on." You may not be that crazy about hand-me-downs or secondhand clothes, but if they're from a friend you might wear them.

Jonathan gave David his clothing! Now, before you get weirded out by that, take a look at what was meant by each of the items that Jonathan gave to David. This story comes from 1 Samuel 18:4, right after David's victory over Goliath. Even early in their relationship, Jonathan must have seen that God's hand was clearly with David: "Jonathan took off the robe he was wearing and gave it to David, along with his tunic, and even his sword, his bow and his belt." So, along with his robe and tunic, or cloak, Jonathan gives David . . .

- His sword. OK, yes, this is actually a cool gift. But it also has great meaning. The sword is a symbol of protection and Jonathan's sword was a picture of Israel's future protection being placed in David's hands. So as Jonathan gives his sword to David he's saying, "I trust you with protecting our great nation of Israel."

- Next came Jonathan's bow and arrows. OK, again, a very cool gift. But again, look at the meaning behind this one. The bow was a sign of strength. It was Jonathan's attempt to make David look good, even above himself. How many friends do you have who you seek to make look better than yourself? Too often, we seek to impress our friends and yet at the same time place ourselves ahead of them.

- Jonathan then gives David his belt. So you may not get all that thrilled about a belt. When was the last time you got a belt as a gift and went crazy over it, right? But this belt was no ordinary belt; it stood for *work*. It was Jonathan saying, "I am giving this belt to you because there is great work to be done and I trust you to do it."

- There was his robe. Not a bathrobe! This was a real, kingly robe that had all types of colors and symbols on it, probably including his family's crest. Such a robe would signify who you were. No doubt Jonathan had a robe that was royal in every way, so it stood out like a sore thumb; anyone who saw it knew this was the king's son's robe. By giving it to David Jonathan was saying, "You are to be the next king." This proves without much doubt that Jonathan knew and heard from God because he gave David what God had earlier prepared and anointed for *him*.

BURST:

BRANDED:

3. The Power of Covering

a. Take the clothes right off my back

Finally, Jonathan gives David his tunic, or garment. At first, this doesn't seem all that interesting—maybe even strange, a little off the normal idea of gift-giving. "Hey, I like you; here's my garments." So what does that mean? Well, in the Scriptures, tunics, or garments, truly were coverings. Here are a few examples of how garments were used in Scripture:

- Psalm 104:2 says that God wraps himself in light as with a garment.

- When Christ entered Jerusalem (Matthew 21:8), the crowds threw down their garments. It was their way of saying, "We've got your back."

- And Jesus' outer garment, or cloak, was the medium through which the hemorrhaging woman was healed. She told herself that if she could just touch the cloak, she would be healed (Matthew 9:20, 21).

In biblical times, garments had deep, significant meanings. Jonathan gave his to David, straight off his own back!

b. I got your back!

Can you imagine what David felt when he received all these gifts? What was it like, and what did he think when Jonathan gave him his garment, his covering? Studying this, you can see how the two were instantly connected to each other. They not only said they were friends, they proved it by their gifts and the sacrifices behind them.

Later in their relationship, in 1 Samuel 23, Jonathan and David met up after David had been hiding from king Saul, Jonathan's father, who had been trying to kill David. **(You may want to read 1 Samuel 23:15-18.)** This is the final recorded time that the two were together. Jonathan encourages David, reminds him that he has his back, makes a covenant with David, and speaks the vision for David's life one more time. They most likely departed thinking that they would one day meet again and renew their friendship. But as the book of Second Samuel unfolds we see a very different story!

David had just returned from a three-day battle and a foot soldier runs to him with some huge news. He tells David that Saul and Jonathan have been killed in battle. What does David do?

He tears his garments! His covering is gone. In one sense, David's more important covering is gone. His best friend, the one who sacrificed the most for him and has given him everything, the one who believed in him and encouraged him and loved him and spoke life to him and protected him . . . gone! That covering for David was now gone!

FOR DISCUSSION:

- Have you had a relationship like that of Jonathan and David? What does a friendship like that mean?

BURST:

BRANDED:

Wrap It Up

It's a great prayer to ask God for a friend like that in your life. But more importantly, _seek to become a friend like that to someone in your life._ Cover them, protect them, love them, encourage them, and speak life to them!

This is what the kingdom of God is about! Friends who are there for one another and have one another's back.

A great prayer is to have a friend of whom you can say, "I've got his back." And for a friend who will be there for *you* and say of you, "I've got her covered."

ALTERED

What's needed: Be ready for action: At the end of this talk, you're going to *tear off your shirt!**; also, *safety pins* and *scissors*

* *Make sure to have a second shirt on underneath.* That way, men, no worries if you haven't been working out! Women leaders: well, we don't have to go there. In all seriousness, having a shirt on underneath is the discreet thing to do.

Also, before the meeting, *pre-tear the shirt a bit* so it will rip easily.

At the end of this talk tear the shirt off your body—literally. But again, you'll have on two shirts, with the outer one a bit pre-torn.

Cut the torn shirt into small pieces and invite group members to come up and take a piece. They can pin it on their clothing or somewhere else they'll see regularly. It will serve as a reminder that they're to be a covering to others in the group.

Encourage your students to spend a few extra minutes talking about how they can be a covering for others.

Option: To make this more impacting, you can tear the shirt off as you tell the story of how David tore his garments at the news of Jonathan's death.

End the night with prayer.

RUNNING WITH SCISSORS (LET GOD DO THE TRIMMING INSTEAD)

WHAT IT'S ALL ABOUT

Since being kids, we've heard this "truth" over and over: running with scissors is dangerous; don't do it! Scissors, though, can provide a picture of just what we need in our lives: we need what keeps us from a close walk with God—sin—cut out of our lives. That's what this message is about: asking God to cut away the things that are keeping us from the fullest life, the best life, the life he wants for us.

Achieving purity before God is a lifelong process, and it starts by allowing him to cut the sin away from our lives. Stress to your students that this is what God wants for them: the best life, a life free from sin.

Get It Started

What's needed: A *small stack of paper*; at least *two pair of scissors* (make sure they're not sharp and watch your students closely as they cut so you don't end up with cut hands; also: stress that this is *not* a race, and you should eliminate any worries)

A simple one, but fun: Pick out a couple of students and hand them a pair of scissors and some paper. It's a contest to see who can cut out the best star! . . . Just one thing. Explain that there's one important rule to this game: they have to do all the cutting behind their backs.

Have your other students judge who cuts the best star. Do a number of pairs of students.

Where It's Found in the Bible

Colossians 2:11

In him you were also circumcised, in the putting off of the sinful nature, not with a circumcision done by the hands of men but with the circumcision done by Christ.

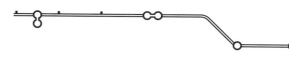

YOUTH TALK OUTLINE

1. Anatomy of a Haircut

a. It must be the scissors—or maybe not

Have you ever seen this? Some of you ladies, or your moms, will pay hundreds of dollars for a cut, curl, and color. You'll sit for hours while it happens—with a smile on your face! When it's over you cry! Why are you crying? Tears of joy and thanksgiving! Guys don't get it, but guys are guys! They don't get much! So anyway, you melt because your new 'do looks *sooooo* good. You can't wait to show your friends, family, and maybe even a certain guy—who won't fully appreciate it, but *will* notice it.

There are guys who go for the great 'do, also. Ever seen some of those high-profile political candidates and their $300 cuts? Yes, even some guys can go crazy over their hair!

So anyway, that new style of yours: was it the scissors that made the difference? Do you think that one cut was great because one pair of scissors is better than another? Of course not. Your stylist is a master at cutting away the old length and leaving you with something that looks extremely happy to your eyes.

BURST:

BRANDED:

b. Some cuts are worth every penny

Here's another thing men are: cheapskates. In fact, some men cut their own hair to save a few bucks. Uhhh, not a good choice. Ladies, on the other hand, know that some things are worth the cost. You get what you pay for—and, after all, you're wearing that thing in front of everyone. So a good cut is worth the cost.

Here's the reality of a life in Christ: It's a life of cuts also. It's a life of pruning and shearing. Jesus tells us that if we expect to grow we also have to expect to get cut. To get pruned. Listen to Jesus' words from John 15:1-4:

"I am the true vine, and my Father is the gardener. He cuts off every branch in me that bears no fruit, while every branch that does bear fruit he prunes so that it will be even more fruitful. You are already clean because of the word I have spoken to you. Remain in me, and I will remain in you."

What great words! He's cleaned us through his life and death, and he desires that we remain in him. But there's also a price to staying pure, to making sure that the bad stuff is cleared from our lives. That price is pruning. That price is a good cut in our lives.

Jesus is clear that he chooses to prune us not because he wants us to hurt or be uncomfortable—but because this is how we grow. Quite the opposite of a great haircut, a good cut in the spiritual realm means there is growth coming in our lives.

Any good caretaker of trees or plants knows all about pruning. It's the process of cutting away the dead, dying, or unfruitful branches or leaves so that real growth can take the place of what's draining resources without bearing fruit.

Have you ever wondered why God cut—or pruned—something out of your life? At different times in our lives, we sit on different sides of God's pruning process.

Some have seen things cut out of their life and don't know why—and maybe hold this against God. Why did you take that friend away? Why did you take that job away? Why did you take that sport, or that position, away? It can seem hard if we only look at what we've lost.

Then there are those who sit on the other side of God's pruning and now see that what God did makes perfect sense. The lesson becomes not about "why didn't I make that cheerleading squad?" but rather what God did to help you grow through that experience. Have you ever known someone who got cut from a team, sport, or organization and yet found it one of the best things to happen to them, who took it all with a great deal of peace? They now recognize something about why God did what he did: Maybe it gives them more time to work on true friendships, or to have meaningful quiet times with God, or that maybe what happened kept them from some pretty unhealthy relationships.

FOR DISCUSSION WITH YOUR GROUP:

- Has God cut something from your life that you didn't understand?
- Have you had God prune away something and now it makes perfect sense why he did?
- How do we gain real peace when God takes away things that we're sure we deserve or can handle—but he does it anyway?

Let's look at cutting from another angle: something a little more intense than just a few hairs on our heads. What if you had to be cut open on an operating table? That's a very uncomfortable experience, but if it saves your life you know it's well worth it. What if your doctor told you that you have cancer and he needs to operate, but that he doesn't want to cut you open, so he's just going to yell through your skin at the cancer to leave? Ridiculous, right? You'd be looking for a new doctor. When it's a matter of life or death any normal person tells the doctor: "Do whatever you need to do. You can cut me head to toe if you have to in order to save my life."

But how many cuts are you willing to take from God so that he can grow your character and make sure you're saved for eternity?

2. Bad Cuts, Good Cuts

a. It keeps coming back!

Back to haircuts: Probably the only thing worse than a bad haircut would be half a haircut. Can you imagine that you're sitting in your chair, your stylist is going great guns, and then she takes a phone call, appears to panic, and rushes out the door.

You're left sitting there with color in your hair or with only half your hair actually cut and there is no one who can finish you. You're forced to go home and wait until your stylist can finish the job. Just be glad you weren't there to get a tattoo!

Our walk with Christ can sometimes look nearly the same way. Really, what would be worse than only having a few destructive things cut out of our lives but leaving all the other similar stuff to grow? God, through the apostle Paul, says in our verse, Colossians 2:11, that we're completely circumcised in and through his work on the cross, his death, and his resurrection. We won't go into circumcision in this setting, but obviously, to the Jews, it meant a cutting away of a part of the body. So Paul was using this picture, to the Colossian Christians, to say that your sinful nature has been cut away. Why would we not want to let God continue that work and get out of our lives what needs to go?

Have you ever seen a little kid getting his hair cut? There he is, squirming, squealing, and desperately wanting to get out of the chair—in the middle of the haircut! We laugh and just wish the kid could understand that he won't get hurt. But shouldn't we ask the question: If we're under God's control and he's circumcised us spiritually through Christ to bring us into a relationship with him, but now he wants to continue to cut sin and distractions away so we can have the best life, why do we squirm and try desperately to get away from what he's doing? Aren't we being a little like that kid in the chair getting his hair cut?

In Colossians 2 the word *circumcision* can be taken to mean, in terms of our relationships, that we've been separated from those who don't love Christ, and from those patterns, habits, and choices that are contrary to him.

FOR DISCUSSION

- If we've been circumcised in Christ, why do we struggle so much with our sinful nature?
- How can we prepare ourselves for God's pruning?

Our sinful nature is constantly tugging at us. Sin is a little like the hair on our heads—both constantly keep coming back. We may think we've dealt with most of the things in our lives, but there will always be more. We can deal with one sin, cut it from our lives, but there are always other areas where sin tries to creep in.

b. It's in God's hands

We all have lots of areas in our lives that need God's pruning power. One mistake we can routinely fall into is trying to cut those areas out on our own. But God says we can turn to him for a good, clean cut, that *he* will take care of it. Jesus said in John 15

RUNNING WITH SCISSORS (LET GOD DO THE TRIMMING INSTEAD)

that if we stay plugged into him—"remain in me," he says—we will continue to grow for God. And here is the secret to this growth pattern: <u>If we're remaining in Jesus by walking with him daily, we're making the decision that we want to grow, that we understand our need for pruning, and we're asking God to actively prune us.</u>

But if you're not remaining in Jesus you won't see the need for his work in your life. It's a little like sitting in a dark room and your excuse for not knowing you're in the dark is that there's not enough light to know it's pitch black! Some people live, spiritually, just like that.

God asks us to trust him, to put our lives in his hands, moment by moment, and to let him have his way.

It's only when we remain in his hands that we see how much work still needs to be done.

BURST:

BRANDED:

3. Cut It Out

a. It's got to go

The human body, although made up of trillions of cells—some say as many as 50 to 75 trillion!—works in a truly amazing, even miraculous, way. Somehow, all those cells work together in harmony to make the body operate in a whole and healthy way.

But there is an exception to the rule and that's the existence of the cancer cell. The cancer cell is the one cell in the body that acts in a completely selfish way, attacking and killing other cells in the body.

When people have malignant cancer cells, what percentage of those cells do they want removed through surgery? It's not hard to guess that the answer is all of them—every last one! Any that are left in the body will continue to spread and eat and destroy the other cells.

So how much sin do you want cut from your spiritual body? Just a little? Or do you want it all taken care of? Here's the deal: you get to choose!

The real questions to ask are: How much will it cost you if you leave sin unchecked? Active cancer can't be left unchecked—it metastasizes; it spreads to other areas of the body, other major organs, and becomes even more deadly. How will that sin affect your life in other areas? Are you willing to take that risk?

BURST:

BRANDED:

b. We've got to grow

But to live the most abundant life, to bear real fruit for God, all we really have to do is walk with Christ and be open to God's pruning. We need to be willing to go to God and say that we need him to cut away the things that we know should be gone.

FOR DISCUSSION:

Note: Here's a chance to let students be vulnerable and share specifics. Hopefully, through the Burst and Branded sections or in some other way, you've first shared about God working in your own life.

Caution: Help students to share, but keep things to generalities and/or encourage sharing of specifics not meant for large groups to be done in small groups later.

- In what areas do you need God's pruning?
- How can we help each other?

Wrap It Up

Spiritually, don't be like that little kid squirming in his chair! Don't seek to get out from under God's pruning! His goal is to mold and shape you into the work of art you were meant to become.

Today we can pray together a simple prayer: "God, I sit here quietly waiting for you to come and cut away at my life. Cut out what keeps me from drawing closer to you. Prune me so that I'm more fruitful for you."

ALTERED

What's needed: *Something from your past that you're willing to cut up* in front of your students

You will lead the way with this activity. Identify something from your past that was a stumbling block and kept you from closely walking with God. Examples: An old high school yearbook that might symbolize how you were all about seeking popularity; an old sports uniform from which you gained most of your self-identity; or maybe something goofy like a pair of old dance shoes because you were so good you could have won *Dancing with the Stars* if they had it back in the day.

Shred or cut this item in front of the students. Explain to them how ten, fifteen—whatever!—years ago it gave you your identity, but years later, God has deepened your perspective in huge ways.

Hand out pieces of this item to your students if you'd like.

Caution: Of course, extracurricular activities are not bad in and of themselves and can be quite healthy. Make sure you set the right tone with this closer. Encourage students that it's great to be involved in organizations and teams—as long as God is God and everything else is not.

Afterward, if your students feel motivated and want to emulate your action, encourage them to talk with you. Help them plan a way to bring in an old uniform next week, or at the next meeting, or to *discreetly* cut a strand of hair, something of that nature. Don't encourage students to gouge their new $80 pair of birthday jeans, or to disfigure their new hairdos. (Trust us, you don't need the parent problems that would come with those actions.) In this case, encourage depth of thought, prayer, and changes in action more than physical actions and symbols.

End the night with prayer.

FILL ME UP
(WITH GOD'S SPIRIT)

WHAT IT'S ALL ABOUT

In the preceding meeting you encouraged your students to allow God to prune, or cut away, the destructive things in their lives. But life has to be about more than just cutting things out, right? What do we *put into* our lives?

Have you ever been driving somewhere and held your breath while you watched your gas gauge plunge to, or below, the empty line? The "low fuel" light comes on and you know you're only miles away from pushing your car if you don't get more gas soon. It's somewhere between "empty" and "running on fumes" that you start to panic.

Our spiritual lives can reflect this same predicament: We're either empty or almost empty. In this meeting you'll tackle the spiritual principle of being continually filled with God's spirit.

Get It Started

What's needed: *four plastic milk jugs (gallon size)*—punch four or five holes in the bottom of each; *four empty trash containers, half-filled with water; four empty five-gallon buckets;* and a *tarp to lay across the floor* if you're going to be inside

This will get messy! The object is simple—and will give you a head start on an illustration for this lesson. Four teams of two students working together will compete against each other by running about 30 feet to a large trash can half-filled with water. They'll fill their milk jug and walk it another 30 feet to a five-gallon bucket. The goal is to do this until the five-gallon bucket is full.

Did you think there might be a catch? Yes, each milk jug should have holes punched in the bottom quarter of the jug; perhaps a couple at the bottom and a few along the sides. Plenty of water should spill out as they run to the bucket.

Some students may catch on to this trick (which you won't tell them, but won't disallow, either): when the jug is filled they can hold the top shut with the palm of their hand and turn the jug upside down and very little will spill out.

Note: This activity is best done outside, but also can be done in a large indoor area that can be easily mopped—choose one or the other if you want to keep your job. If indoors, you'll want to make sure your students aren't slipping; make it a rule that they can only walk with the filled water jug.

Where It's Found in the Bible

Ephesians 5:17, 18

Therefore do not be foolish, but understand what the Lord's will is.

Do not get drunk on wine, which leads to debauchery. Instead, be filled with the Spirit.

YOUTH TALK OUTLINE

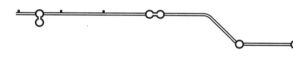

1. Running on Empty

    a. "We're on E!"

You have the perfect day planned. It starts with a beautiful cruise through the countryside to the beach, where you'll unpack your picnic baskets and you and your friends will eat, laugh, and swim. You'll get a tan and play great tunes and take pictures on your cell phone to post on your Web site. This will go down in history as the perfect day.

However, if you miss just one detail it will all come crashing down. That little detail is the gas needed for your ride; did you make sure you have enough? You can have the convertible, the lunch, the swimsuit, and the tunes with the perfect playlist, but if you don't have enough gas you'll be sitting roadside counting the cars as they whiz by.

It would be pretty foolish to take off knowing you're on empty, right? People would think there's something else on empty and it's what sits above your neck.

We're all built with a spiritual fuel tank as well. It's inside of us and we can't see it but we can definitely feel it and we know when it's pushing empty.

You can't get gas while driving your car down the road; you have to pull over, get out, and fill up. Our spiritual fuel tanks need the same kind of care and caution. The world is very draining, so every day you have to be willing to stop and fill up so you can get where God wants you to go. Too many people are pushing their cars around when God is there to provide a fuel that will get us where we need to go. So what is the fuel we should fill our inner beings with? The real question is *who* is the fuel we should be filling up with. We'll get to that shortly. But first, you have to see the need to be filled, to go after the right fuel source. When we don't tap into that source, we're being foolish, as Paul wrote to the Ephesians.

BURST:

BRANDED:

b. Are fumes really OK?

Have you ever pulled up to the pump and ravaged the ash tray, tore up things under the seat, and maybe even scoured through your trunk for a few extra coins to total up to a dollar or two to put into your tank? So you put in a buck-fifty and take off merrily down the road, but you're still really operating on fumes. You can't go far. Most people—except for those Type A, everything-in-its-place people—have experienced something like this in owning a car. You've pushed things to the limit and hoped and prayed that you'll make it even while your car's on empty. Your prayer life may have gotten stronger as mile after mile went by. But not exactly what God has in mind for us to grow in prayer!

The good news is that God doesn't call us to run on fumes; he wants us to have a full spiritual tank. Too often, even as followers of Christ, we go day after day thinking it's OK to live life on an empty spiritual tank, essentially running on fumes. Here's the really good news: God's called us to not only run on full but to run on overflowing. He wants us to have an abundance of life and of his Spirit. He wants us to have the best life. Why is it that so many people look at Christians and don't see any real difference between themselves and the so-called Christ-followers? You can't follow Christ to the full if you're running on empty spiritually. People are attracted to those who have the abundant life that Jesus talked about in John 10:10.

FOR DISCUSSION WITH YOUR GROUP:

- Can you recall a time you ran on empty spiritually? Can you share? What was the outcome?
- Have you lived in such a way that you were filled with God's Spirit? What victories did God give you? What were you able to accomplish?

2. The Right Way to Get Drunk

a. It's got to be with the Spirit!

From time to time we've all chosen to run after things that prove quite intoxicating. We choose lots of different things: school, sports, relationships, pleasure, other means of self-fulfillment, and maybe even alcohol or drugs. Anything that you try to fill your tank with that's not God's Spirit will provide a fleeting fulfillment.

Today, is God tapping you on the shoulder to let you know you're filling up on the wrong fuel? Imagine the stares you'd get if you pulled into a gas station and instead of putting gas in your tank you poured in windshield wiper fluid. Hey, you like the cool blue color, it doesn't stink like gas, and it's way cheaper. But a few miles down the road your car is going to sputter and die.

Spiritually, is that you, or are you filling up with God's Spirit?

b. Debaucha—what?

We have to look at one more thing to avoid. What is this *debauchery* that Paul talks about? It's defined as "extreme indulgence for sensual pleasure." Paul says that drunkenness is debauchery, and there are many other forms of debauchery as well. This sin leads to weakness and emptiness and a person finally just give ups or gets lost in life. How many people look back in life and wonder where it all fell apart?

Putting this all together, we can see that whatever we fill our lives with determines how far we go in our walk with God.

So ask yourself tonight: Are you running on empty, are you running on a full tank, or are you not sure?

BURST:

BRANDED:

3. Fill 'Er Up

a. With the Spirit

Maybe you have a dad who goes to the gas station to fill up and, once the tank is full, he just can't help but try to top it off. (Even though most pumps say, "Do not top off!") So there goes Dad: Dribble, click—dribble, click—dribble, click . . . and finally it spurts back out all over his shoes and you have to smell it the rest of the way to where you're going.

Believe it or not, this is how God wants us to live! He wants us to be full, and overflowing, so that others can smell what—or who—is flowing out of us: God's Holy Spirit.

How much is enough? How much of God's Spirit do you want from day to day? We should want all we can get and then some. In fact, God says this is his will; this is what he wants for you.

Here's another Dad picture, but a good one: You pull your car up to fill up your tank but you only have a few dollars. Your Dad steps over, hands you his credit card, and says, "I want you to fill it all the way up." Then he gives you the credit card for good and says you can use it to fill your car whenever you'd like.

That's what God wants to do for you! That's God's will for you today. The *who* of this fuel God wants to give you is the Holy Spirit. *He* is a Spirit who wants to stay with you and guide you. Do a study on as many verses as you can find about the Holy Spirit. Here are just a few:

- Jesus said of the Spirit: "You know him, for he lives with you and will be in you" (John 14:17).
- Jesus said he "will teach you all things and will remind you of everything I have said to you" (John 14:26).
- Romans 8:26 says he "helps us in our weakness" and even helps us pray when we don't know the right words to say. How cool is that?
- And the very next verse says the Spirit intercedes with God for us, and this statement comes after assurance that God searches our hearts as he tries to strengthen us.

FOR DISCUSSION:

- How has God's Spirit helped you? At times, this isn't easy to understand, or easily explainable. But we have to be aware of the ways God is working in us through his Spirit.

- Romans 8:27 says the Spirit intercedes for us—but his working must be in accordance with God's will. How can we know when God's trying to work in our lives through the Spirit?
- When might we wonder that something taking place in our lives is *not* God's will and *not* what the Spirit wants to do?

b. To the point of overflowing

If you want to make sure that you spill something on yourself, do this one thing: Put on the cleanest, whitest shirt you have. Guaranteed, spillage will occur!

God wants spillage in your life—he wants you full and overflowing! It's not enough to go through life for ourselves only—God wants us to live to benefit others as well. When life takes a swing at you and knocks you down, what will come spilling out? If you're filled with his Spirit, then that is what will come bubbling out.

BURST:

BRANDED:

Wrap It Up

During our opening activity some of you may have realized there was a trick you could do. The gallon jugs had holes in the bottom that allowed the water to spill out, but if you turned the jugs upside down and covered the opening then you could keep more water inside. We have to place our lives upside down from the way the world does things to keep them filled. God says to go the opposite direction from where the world is pointing, to do things his way, and though it may seem backward at first and maybe even upside down, you'll find that you stay filled longer.

The world says: "Stay busy! Run after things that are intoxicating!" God says, "Slow down. Be filled with my Spirit."

Sure, you'll have to continually lean on God for filling, but that's what life with God's Spirit is about. And this is the best life, the life he desires for you.

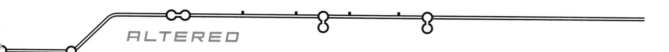

ALTERED

What's needed: Some quiet or otherwise reflective *mood music*, if you wish

Break your students up into groups of three to five—no bigger, if possible. Make them guys and girls groups; don't mix.

Give the groups ten to fifteen minutes to discuss how they can slow down, experience God more, and listen to and rely on the Spirit. An extremely difficult thing for all us, even adults and church leaders! In addition to those thoughts, give them three questions to consider:

- Reflect on the John 14:26 verse: How can we allow the Spirit to teach us and remind us of the things Christ taught us?
- Discuss how the Spirit has helped us in times of weakness and how he can help us in the future (your students might anticipate some upcoming trials or challenges in their lives).
- What does a life overflowing with the Spirit look like? It's important to encourage your students that that doesn't necessarily mean loud, hyper, or busy! How does the Spirit manifest himself in our lives?

Project these questions for your students or make copies of them ahead of time.

End the night with prayer.

THE BIBLE, THE BOND
(TRUST WHERE GOD IS LEADING)

WHAT IT'S ALL ABOUT

Most youth pastors want their students to know how committed they are to seeing them grow in Christ. Growth is dependent on prayer, reading Scripture, and Christian fellowship. But for better or worse, Christian leadership also can make a huge impact on the growth of the members in the youth group.

As a youth leader whom students look to for guidance and leadership in many ways, you'll use this meeting to share your vision and commitment to your group. This vision should include preaching God's Word, praying for your students, and being there for them both in times of struggle and celebration.

Get It Started

What's needed: *A talk—and practice this activity!—with other leaders and volunteers beforehand; a table* to stand on

(Practicing this a few times before your students arrive is a necessary thing. Nothing kills an activity meant to illustrate trust like someone involved breaking the trust!)

If you're a fan of the show *24* you've heard the hero, Jack Bauer, utter these words what seems like hundreds of times: "You're going to have to trust me." These can be powerful words, especially coming from a youth pastor or leader who's been charged by God to watch over young people. It's powerful to both give and receive trust.

You and the other leaders will give your students a demonstration that provides a small symbol of trustworthy leadership.

As the leader, you do this first: Stand on a table with your back to the group of other leaders. They will stand below you and link arms. When the leaders say, "Fall!", do just that, trusting your leadership to catch you.

Then have another leader or two do the same as a symbol of saying that your leadership is trustworthy.

Option: Drop the table idea; just do this from a standing position

Where It's Found in the Bible

2 Timothy 4:1-3

In the presence of God and of Christ Jesus, who will judge the living and the dead, and in view of his appearing and his kingdom, I give you this charge: Preach the Word; be prepared in season and out of season; correct, rebuke and encourage—with great patience and careful instruction. For the time will come when men will not put up with sound doctrine. Instead, to suit their own desires, they will gather around them a great number of teachers to say what their itching ears want to hear.

YOUTH TALK OUTLINE

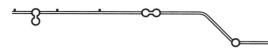

1. Who Do You Trust?

a. The ABCs of trust

Almost everyone wants to be trusted, and there is some hurt when we don't feel the trust of other significant people in our lives (whether we caused that lack of trust or not). A funny thing happens when we're passionate about someone or something: we want to be trusted. A lot of youth leaders might forget to take the dog out—even if the poor thing is sitting there whining and has its legs crossed—but if you asked them to meet with a student or lead a small group or preach a sermon, that's something they won't forget. They're passionate about seeing young people grow in Christ—and that is the leadership that God wants for you.

I think this is what we see in the words from the apostle Paul to Timothy in this text in Second Timothy. You can just hear his heart beat through the pages as he encourages Timothy to do his best to grow the church. And when people are passionate and serve others out of that passion, trust comes far more easily.

We want you to know your leadership is passionate about serving you and this church. And about living out what is said in these verses, including the reading and preaching of Scripture, making the understanding of Scripture challenging and fun, and engaging in life with you. Youth pastors and leaders actually like doing things like preparing a calendar and planning activities that will stretch the group members in areas of discipleship, worship, service, and fellowship. They love correcting, rebuking, and encouraging—and doing it with great patience and careful instruction.

It's not always easy, but they love doing it. And they want others to learn from the mistakes they've made before them.

BURST:

BRANDED:

b. Pain before prosperity

Ever had a blood test or donated blood? Think about what a phlebotomist does. (And yes, that's always a fun word to say; far more fun to say than to experience one doing their job!) Anyway, think of it: They get paid to stick people with big, long, sharp needles. What a job! But someone has to do this job, and the taking of blood is one way to find out if you're healthy or in need of treatments of some type.

Leaders in the church have to do the same sort of thing for the same sort of reason. They sometimes have to initially cause pain—and there is nothing enjoyable about that—to help people find ways to get to healthier places in their lives. It's not easy rebuking, correcting, or preaching the hard stuff out of Scripture—but it is needed. It is part of God's plan to bring us to the best place in life. In the same way, no one really wants that needle stuck in their arm, but it just may be the first step to saving their life. Do you think many nurses have people go back to them and say, "Thanks for sticking that ugly, pointy, painful needle in my arm! I really appreciate it." Probably very few!

As youth leaders, we often don't get a lot of thanks for the hard stuff, either. Leaders do what they do because they love people—God wants you to be assured of that, and God wants *you* to have a vision for serving others in the same way.

Leaders are charged by God to do the things listed in this Scripture—but they always should do them out of love and concern, and we want you to hold us accountable to that. If a leader in the church—youth leader or otherwise—doesn't live up to the things God has charged him or her to do, he or she will be held accountable!

FOR DISCUSSION WITH YOUR GROUP:

- Why is it hard for people to trust?
- Why do we tend to run from things that are painful or difficult?
- Why is it sometimes hard to trust leaders (in or out of the church)?
- How can we grow in trust that leadership will say things that challenge us or make us feel uncomfortable only because they have our ultimate good in mind?
- In what ways can you trust that this is God's plan?

2. A Charge from God

a. If it's in the game, it's in the game

Have you ever tried learning a new game with some friends, but just about the time you think you've figured it out they keep changing the rules? You win $10 only to find out that because it's Tuesday and you have on red socks you have to give what you won to the person on the right. *What?*, you think. *Where did that rule come from? I'm out of here!* You never quite know what's coming next and you feel like you'll never stand a chance at winning the game with all these new or surprise rules. So you're like, "If it's in the rules, tell me. If it's in the rules, it's in the rules. Stop changing them on me!"

Imagine being in a youth ministry in which no one wanted to give to you straight the real rules God has for life. <u>Lots of people fail miserably at life because no one told them all the rules—the real, godly ways to live and how to make it spiritually. As your leaders, we don't want to be that person or that leadership group.</u> God wants your leaders to be trustworthy, and he wants them to teach you his rules for life. All of them.

The goal of your leaders is that you build your faith on solid rock, not sand, and they want to give you the tools needed to build in that way. **(Option: Read Matthew 7:24-27.)**

BURST:

BRANDED:

b. Prepared to prepare

Have you ever had a guide? Maybe it was a guide for a hiking trip, for climbing, traveling, sightseeing, or just to get you from one side of the Super Wal-Mart to the other. When hiking, a good guide is prepared for what you're not prepared for. You may want to start a fire, check your direction, or cover up from the elements, and you may not be prepared to do those things—but your guide will. He may know what you don't about why not to start that fire at that time in that location.

In his letter, Paul told Timothy to be prepared "in season and out of season." This is not just for Timothy's sake; it's for the sake of the church members whom he oversees.

And God's given the same charge to your leaders.

We take that charge seriously. We have to be prepared in order to make sure you are prepared. So how do you prepare for someone else's preparation? Just like the apostle Paul said, a leader *must* read Scripture, give strong instruction, teach sound doctrine, correct, and be wise and careful in how they live and do their job. They must prepare themselves first and then prepare to prepare others!

FOR DISCUSSION:

- If you were to go out today and try to guide someone through the mountains, would you be prepared to do that job? If not, how would you prepare?
- How should a leader in God's church prepare for his?

Most of us probably wouldn't be prepared to guide someone through the mountains! We'd need a guide who has been there and done that.

Your youth leaders are here to guide you through this stage in your life! Whoever they are, an element of trust is needed, as well as an element of learning from their example as they try to teach you from their mistakes and guide and prepare you for your journey!

c. Leaving a mark

If you've ever channel-surfed there's a good chance you've come across one of many shows about tattoos and other body art. It's always interesting to see what people will put on their bodies and for what reason. There once was a show about a woman who put the paw prints of her dog on her calf—all four paws. She said it was so she would always remember him. Can you imagine loving a pet that much?

Some people need helps to remember the things that are most important to them. God has given your leaders a solemn charge—to serve, love, encourage, and

move you closer to Christ and heaven. A tattoo shouldn't be needed. These things are always on their hearts. This charge from God has left a permanent mark.

Wrap It Up

Your youth leaders are charged by God to take their jobs seriously. Will you trust them?

Will you take your charge from God seriously? Will you prepare for the day when you are leading others?

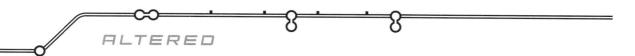

ALTERED

Warning: Do this Altered only if you're prepared to stay in your job for, at the very least, the next year.

What's needed: *A new Bible*

At the end of this talk invite your students to come up front and sign their names on your new Bible—front cover, back cover, inside cover, whatever you and they want.

Give them your word that you will use this Bible for the next year as a reminder to pray diligently and serve them with the solemn charge given you by God.

End the night with prayer.

FAITH PARTY
(THE FUTURE IS BRIGHT)

WHAT IT'S ALL ABOUT

Where will you be in five years? How about ten? As much as it's good and healthy to set goals and go after them, none of us really knows the answers to those questions, do we?

Faith Party is a youth talk that looks into the future with faith. This meeting will be tons of fun as you get to share your vision for the ministry, the students, and the church.

But more importantly, they get to dream about theirs. So here's what you do: Before this meeting mail invitations to every student, or get on every Facebook or MySpace page and give invitations. Follow up with texts to all students to reiterate the message. Ask them to come to the next meeting dressed and acting as they want to dress and act in ten years. Through the invitation, help your students by providing some ideas, and invite them to call or visit you or another leader if they need help with their vision for self or with ideas.

Get It Started

What's needed: This one takes a little work but is worth it. First, *mail the invitations as suggested* from the section above; next, *take time to surf the Internet and find pictures of fashions from by-gone eras* (Victorian, Roaring '20s, '50s greasers, and more) and *fashions that experts predict will be "in" many years in the future*

The activity to start the night: show these to your group and see if your students can guess the era they came from.

Option: You may even want to throw in a few pictures of yourself and other leaders from the past or, if you're ambitious, dress up in old clothing.

Ministry idea: You may want to ask an adult—a parent or someone from the community—to share a testimony of how God's vision for their life changed their future and how they saw themselves many years ago. This can really add a punch to the night.

Where It's Found in the Bible

Matthew 9:28, 29

When he had gone indoors, the blind men came to him, and he asked them, "Do you believe that I am able to do this?"

"Yes, Lord," they replied.

Then he touched their eyes and said, "According to your faith will it be done to you."

YOUTH TALK OUTLINE

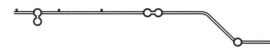

1. What Do You See?

a. Mirror, mirror

The fun house is that one attraction at the fair where you and your friends go inside and run around, nonstop, laughing all the way through—until you stumble into the room of mirrors. That's when you slow down. The room has mirrors that are so distorted, twisted, and angled that you look like the elephant man or, worse yet, your old science teacher. Wide bodies, tiny heads, and your feet have never looked so small. But the one thing you know—thankfully—is that what you're seeing is not reality. The only thing that would be worse is thinking you look better in those mirrors than in yours at home!

We all have a type of mirror in our heads that tells us what we look like, and it's better at telling our future than the mirrors in our bathrooms. When you look into your own personal mirror, what do you see around the next corner? Who will you be and where will your life go?

Everyone puts faith in some type of mirror into their lives. You can't help but believe that you are going to become something in the future. But what's reflecting from your personal mirror? Who do you believe you will be?

BURST:

BRANDED:

b. Harder to see than we think

There is some type of mirror around every corner in our lives. There's the *friend mirror* that reflects who we think we will be based on what our friends think. There's the *parent mirror*—usually, it's even bigger than the friend mirror. There are all kinds of other mirrors. You have what we read on the Internet, listen to in music, see on TV or in movies, hear from our teachers or coaches, or read in magazines.

And then there is your own inner voice; it too reflects pictures of who you're "supposed to be." Even worse is that we often find ourselves trying to live up to—or down to—the expectations of the most critical people in our lives. So that bully at school makes fun of us, and we change to appease him when we really don't even like him! Why should we care what he thinks?

All of this can make it pretty hard to see who we really are.

What about the *God mirror?* We're actually called to reflect the image of God in all we think and do. What Genesis 1:27 says is so important: "So God created man in his own image, in the image of God he created him; male and female he created them." But maybe our God mirror is a little foggy or scratched and we don't quite see ourselves the way God does.

Have you ever gone through your day and finally stumbled onto a mirror and thought, *This is how I look?!?* Maybe you get a little embarrassed and head to the nearest bathroom to water down your hair or tuck in your shirt, or even run home to change.

But how would you change if you saw how God sees you every day?

FOR DISCUSSION WITH YOUR GROUP:

- What mirrors, or measures, do you use to view yourself?
- What's the danger in using mirrors from popular culture and not what the Bible says?
- Let's carry out some discussion on that last point: How would you change if you saw how God truly sees you every day?
- How do you think God sees you?

2. Believe and Then You Will See

a. Do you believe?

In the Matthew 9 passage, Jesus asks an interesting question to some men who are blind. He asks them if they *believe*. Now remember, they can't see Jesus and they obviously have not seen any of his miracles. So to ask them if they believe is a huge question. Jesus is asking them if they believe in something they've never seen and saying that if they do believe, *then* they will see. Pretty ironic. God asks us the same question every time we read his Word or pray with meaning or hear a sermon . . . do we believe in what we can't see? If we believe, we will see.

Have you ever heard a sermon or read Scripture that speaks of who you are in Christ and thought . . . *Hmmmm, not me. God, you must be talking about someone else.* When you do that, you may be just like the blind men in Matthew 9. God is asking you to believe what you can't yet see.

So will you start believing?

FOR DISCUSSION:

- Is that you? Do you hear God say he made you in his image and yet struggle to believe it? Do you say to yourself, he must be talking about someone else?
- Why do so many people do that? Do you struggle with that?
- How can we change that thinking and help each other change?

b. We're all a little blind

Did you know that we have to admit that we're blind before we can begin to see? This is what Jesus said: "For judgment I have come into this world, so that the blind will see and those who see will become blind" (John 9:39).

We're all a little blind as to who we are and who we can become. What Jesus says here, very simply, is, "Admit that you are blind. Let *me* show you how to see. I'll fill in the blind spots in your life."

A wise man once said that it may be that we ask young people the wrong question when we ask, "What do you want to be when you grow up?" Or at least that, we don't follow that question up properly when they get older. When we reach the stage of being young adults, maybe we should ask ourselves this question: "What do I want to be when I die?" Think about the power of knowing what God wants you to be when you die: If you could know today what God wants you to be by the time of your death, then that knowledge would transcend your daily life and you'd begin to make choices to become that man or woman. You could say that would fill in the blind spots of your spiritual walk in a whole new way.

BURST:

BRANDED:

3. How to See Your Future

a. The master's touch

Have you ever had a parent or friend rub your scalp, received a great massage, or had a great foot rub? Heaven, right? Touch is a powerful thing. Touch can soothe muscles, relieve stress, dissipate wrinkles, calm the agitated, and even relieve depression. But Jesus has even more power in his touch than we could imagine. He healed the blind, sick, and demon-possessed. Jesus reached out his hand and calmed the seas. He picked up the guard's ear that Peter sliced off in the Garden of Gethsemane and placed it back onto his head. Even a woman who touched his cloak was healed! That's a man with a powerful touch! The touch of the living Christ is so powerful that it can change eternity.

If God could touch your eyes today and let you see your future and who you are *in him*, would you welcome that gift? What do you think you would see? Do you think it's possible for God to do that for you today?

BURST:

BRANDED:

b. The master's mirror

Today is the day to ask God to give you *his* mirror into the future. That mirror will point you to the prescription of faith. Here are some great ways to see yourself as God sees you:

- Take time to write down verses that you believe God wants to make real in your life.
- Ask others to pray with you and share what God is saying about your life.
- Find out what you're good at and ask God to show you how he wants to use your gifts.

It all comes down to putting aside the mirrors you've been using and using God's mirror into your life instead. When you see who God has created you to be it will make it far easier to live out who God has in mind for you to be—and to become that person.

Wrap It Up

Resist the urge to use the mirrors the world is using. Don't do it! Get God's vision for your life. Don't listen to people who try to get you to see yourself in a different way than God sees you. They want you to see your life the way they see it or the way the world sees it. Again, don't do it. Smash those mirrors!

Who do you want to be, what do you want to have accomplished, on the day you die? It's up to you—and God, with his help—to go out and live that life by faith.

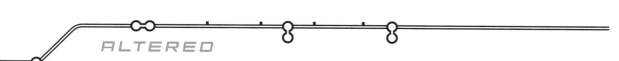

ALTERED

What's needed: A *camera* ready for lots of pictures

The memories have already been made as students have shown up dressed for the future and listened to this message. Now let the students who want to stand up and share with others why they're dressed the way they are and what it means to them.

At the end of the night take lots of pictures and display them on the walls of your youth room or on your student ministry Web site as a reminder both of this meeting and of who your students will be—in Christ.

End the night with prayer.

1. www.winstonchurchill.org/i4a/pages/index.cfm?pageid=423 (accessed November 18, 2008)

2. Isabel Maxey Dittemore, *He Leadeth Me: Forty Years in Asia* (Joplin, Mo., College Press), 17.